On This Day In

SOUTH DAKOTA HISTORY

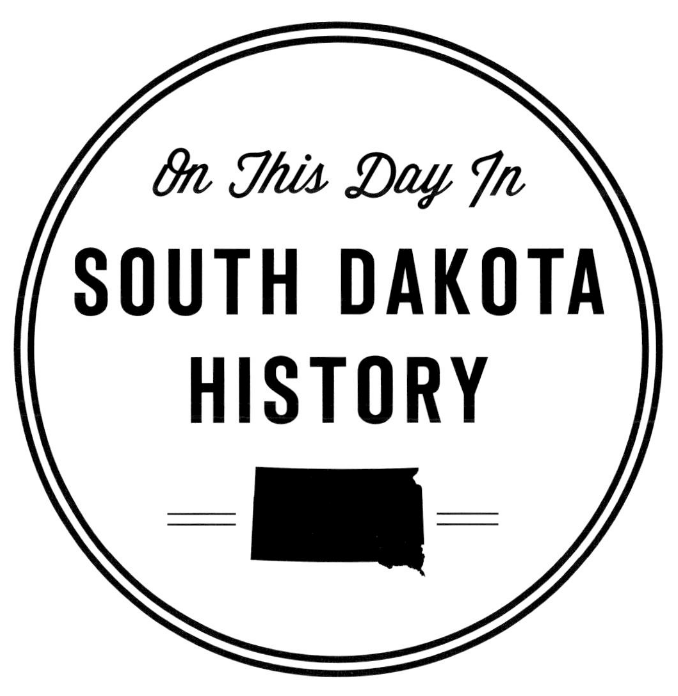

BRAD TENNANT

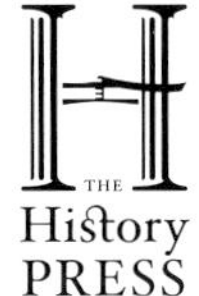

Published by The History Press
Charleston, SC
www.historypress.net

Front cover, top row, left: photo by W.R. Cross, courtesy of Pioneer Museum; *right*: Brad Tennant; *second row, left*: Brigid Tennant; *right*: South Dakota State Historical Society; *third row, left*: public domain as a work of the U.S. Marine Corps; *right*: Jaret Copeman/Sydney Johnson; *fourth row, left*: Brigid Tennant; *right*: photo courtesy of Gabe Raba.
Back cover, top: Jaret Copeman/Sydney Johnson; *bottom*: photo courtesy of Gabe Raba.

First published 2017

Manufactured in the United States

ISBN 9781467119351

Library of Congress Control Number: 2016961717

Notice: The information in this book is true and complete to the best of our knowledge. It is offered without guarantee on the part of the author or The History Press. The author and The History Press disclaim all liability in connection with the use of this book.

Contents

Acknowledgements

The history of South Dakota can be found in a variety of books, newspapers and websites and in numerous archives and museums. This work touched on only a few of the many available sources that exist. In some cases, I knew where to look, and in others, I either depended on those who offered assistance or hoped to get lucky in my research efforts. I often read about one topic that then led me to yet another.

Among those whom I would like to specifically acknowledge are Lauri Langland of the Dakota Wesleyan Archives, Chelle Somsen and Matthew Reitzel of the South Dakota State Archives, Peggy Sanders, Matthew Guthmiller, Sydney Johnson and the editors and staff of The History Press.

In addition to those already mentioned, I want to especially acknowledge my wife, Brigid, whose sense of adventure in traveling and enjoyment in taking photographs contributed to this work. Brigid would often think of events and check to see if I thought they were worthy of mention. In most cases, they were. Furthermore, she is a wonderful travel companion, and we often brainstormed lists of events whenever we traveled around the state.

Introduction

When first contacted about doing this book, I immediately began thinking of some of the more notable events that are but a small part of the overall history of South Dakota. Of course, some stand out as being more significant than others; however, I did not want to make this a work of trivial information. Rather, my goal was to include events that truly shaped the history of South Dakota and beyond. Indeed, many readers may be surprised by how much the history of South Dakota reflects on major national and even international events. For instance, the state's history is also a part of westward settlement, Populism and the Cold War era.

By design, I intentionally focused on events that occurred only since statehood in 1889 or were relevant to the statehood movement. Since Dakota Territory experienced several boundary changes from its creation in 1861 until its end in 1889, I wanted to avoid mentioning some major events of the territorial period but not others. However, I attempted to include events that occurred in different parts of the state. Of course, South Dakota's history cannot be told without including the Lakota, Dakota and Nakota peoples from whom the state gets its name, meaning "friend."

I took special care in checking and double-checking dates, and there were some occasions in which the dates varied by a day or even two. In some cases, there were major discrepancies, but in such instances, I sought to find multiple references. Despite my efforts to substantiate dates, I take responsibility for any errors. I realize that many major events are not included in this work that are certainly worthy of mention. So much history, so little time. I hope you enjoy learning more about the people, places and events that were a part of what took place *On This Day in South Dakota History*.

January

In John Neihardt's *Black Elk Speaks*, he provides Lakota meanings to the months of the Gregorian calendar. Although the Lakota traditionally have a thirteen-month lunar calendar, Neihardt matched the Lakota meanings with the western calendar as he best understood from Black Elk. In the case of January, it would be known as "Moon of Frost in the Tepee." As this is the first full month of winter in South Dakota, the meaning is certainly appropriate. At the same time, January is a month that brings hope and promise for a new year. The first month of the year had some notable firsts, such as the first Lakota congressman and the first Democratic governor. It was also a month during which a state treasurer absconded with South Dakota's treasury, leaving the young state in a serious situation.

January 1, 1974

The Earth Resources Observation and Science (EROS) Data Center, about fifteen miles north of Sioux Falls, officially begins operations at its new facility, which was dedicated in August 1973. EROS is one of the largest computer facilities used by the United States Geological Survey, a bureau of the U.S. Department of the Interior. It has grown from a small staff to approximately six hundred government and contracted employees.

January 2, 1942

As the United States enters World War II, the U.S. War Department establishes Rapid City Army Air Base for training Flying Fortress crews. In September 1942, the base began using its first runways. Although its operations and name underwent changes since its creation, Ellsworth Air Force Base, as it is currently known, played a crucial role throughout the Cold War and is currently the home for the Twenty-Eighth Bomb Wing and one of the nation's largest B-1 bases in the air force. Today, Ellsworth Air Force Base is also home to the South Dakota Air and Space Museum.

January 3, 1961

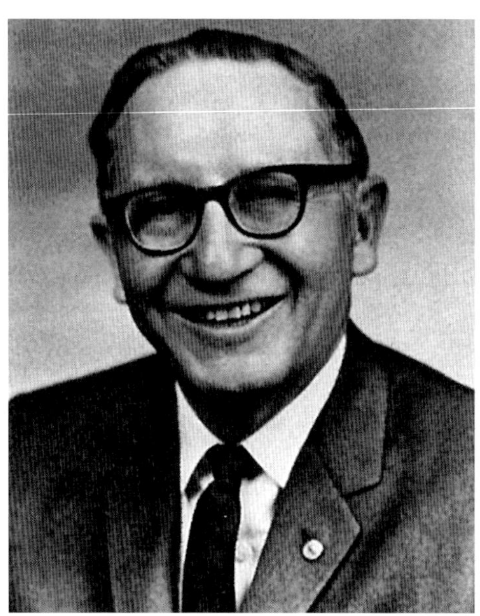

Congressman Ben Reifel. *Collection of the U.S. House of Representatives.*

Republican Ben Reifel begins serving his first term in the U.S. House of Representatives. He never lost an election for South Dakota's First Congressional District and stepped down as a representative after his fifth term in office. Reifel's mother was Lakota, and his father was of German descent, making him the first person of Lakota descent to serve in Congress. Reifel grew up on the Rosebud Indian Reservation and later earned a master's degree and a PhD from Harvard University, where his studies focused on economics and government. In addition to his public service as a congressman, Reifel served in World War II, achieving the rank of lieutenant colonel. He worked for the Department of the Interior and was an administrator for the Bureau of Indian Affairs. Some highlights of his career include supporting the location of the Earth Resources Observation and Science (EROS) Center in South

Dakota, ensuring that Ellsworth Air Force Base remain an active military base, improving the Sioux Falls veterans' hospital and helping establish the National Endowment for the Humanities. He promoted better relations between South Dakota's Indian and non-Indian populations and sought to improve the educational opportunities for Indian youth on reservations.

January 4, 1927

William J. Bulow, South Dakota's twelfth governor and the state's first Democratic governor, assumes office. Rural agricultural states, such as South Dakota, began experiencing a depressed economy beginning in the early 1920s. As economic conditions worsened throughout the decade, voters turned away from the Republican Party in hopes that the Democratic Party would provide greater assistance.

January 5, 2015

Justice Janine Kern joins Justice Lori Wilbur on the South Dakota State Supreme Court, marking the first time two women served on the court simultaneously. Governor Dennis Daugaard appointed both Wilbur and Kern to the five-member court. In 2002, Governor William Janklow appointed Justice Judith Meierhenry, making her the first woman to serve on the South Dakota Supreme Court.

January 6

1911

The first train arrives in Faith. Faith began as a railroad town, was established in 1910 and formally incorporated in 1912 after settlement increased due to the arrival of the railroad in 1911. The origin of the town's name is not certain. Some believe that early settlers chose the name because of the faith it took to live on the northern plains, where winters were cold and harsh and summers were hot and dry. Others believe that the name came from Faith Rockefeller, the daughter of Milwaukee Railroad investor Nelson Rockefeller.

2012

A South Dakota Highway Patrol stop for speeding east of Rapid City results in nearly a half-ton of marijuana being seized. A highway patrol drug unit dog detected what turned out to be 980 pounds of pot with an estimated street value of $3.9 million. Authorities believed that it may be the state's biggest pot bust resulting from a traffic stop.

January 7, 1995

William Janklow begins his third of four terms as governor. Beginning with South Dakota's gaining statehood in 1889 through the 1972 gubernatorial election, governors served two-year terms. Voters approved a state constitutional amendment in 1972 stipulating that governors are elected for four-year terms and are limited to two consecutive terms. Janklow served two consecutive terms from January 1, 1979, to January 6, 1987, and two more consecutive terms from January 7, 1995, to January 3, 2003. He thus has the distinction of serving as the state's twenty-seventh and thirtieth governor. His sixteen years is the longest stint of any governor in South Dakota history.

January 8, 2016

Attorney General Marty Jackley announces that South Dakota has joined Arkansas, Kansas, Michigan, Montana, Nebraska, North Dakota, Ohio, South Carolina and Wyoming in a lawsuit objecting to President Barrack Obama's directive regarding the use of school locker rooms and bathrooms by transgender students. Jackley stated that the lawsuit had been filed with a Nebraska Federal District Court against the U.S. Department of Education and the U.S. Department of Justice.

January 9

1895

Outgoing state treasurer William Walter Taylor (aka Walter William Taylor) leaves South Dakota with $367,020.59 of the state's money and heads for Central America. Taylor eventually surrendered to authorities, and he was brought back to South Dakota, where he received an eighteen-month sentence in the penitentiary. After his arrest, the state was able to recover about $100,000. Unfortunately, South Dakota's first governor, Arthur C. Mellette, served as a bondsman for Taylor. As a result, Mellette suffered a tremendous financial loss while attempting to replace the stolen funds.

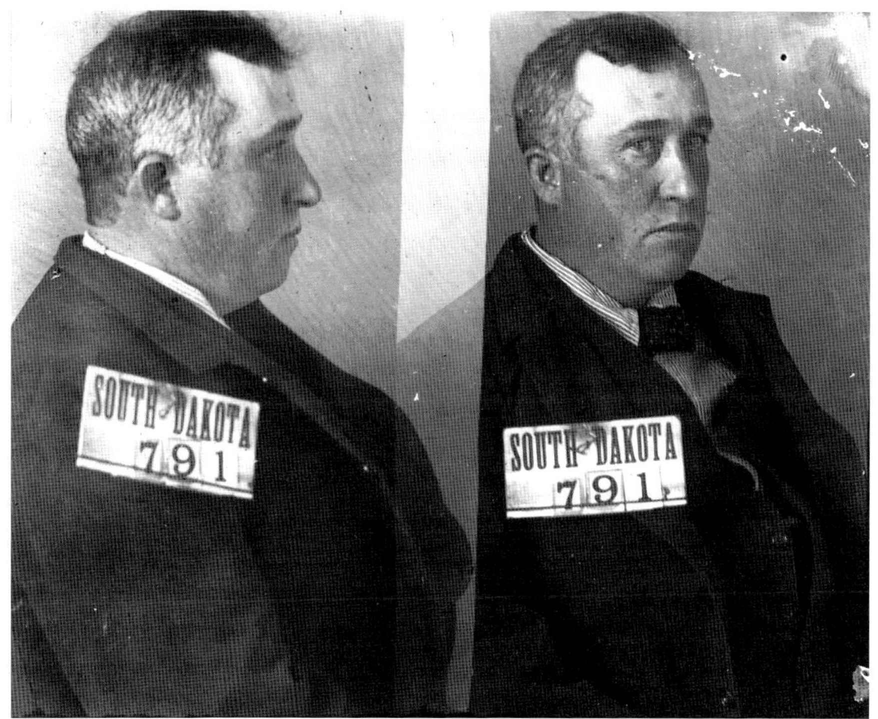

State treasurer William Walter Taylor (aka Walter William Taylor). *South Dakota State Historical Society.*

1903

Wind Cave in the Black Hills is established as the country's eighth national park and the first national park in the world to recognize and protect a cave. Although Wind Cave is one of the country's oldest national parks, it has long been held as sacred by the Lakota people, who have an oral tradition of their arrival to this world from Wind Cave.

January 10, 1949

Secretary of the Interior J.A. Krug issues an order amending earlier orders from June 18, 1934, and June 12, 1941, restoring certain surplus lands on the Cheyenne River Sioux Reservation to tribal ownership. Much of the reservation land had been opened for non-Indian settlement, and the 1934 Indian Reorganization Act, along with the 1941 and 1949 amended orders, sought to reestablish Cheyenne River Sioux tribal land.

January 11, 1969

Four Augustana College debate students and their coach die when their plane, piloted by an Augustana librarian, encounters severe winter weather on their return from a tournament in Colorado Springs, Colorado. Despite attempts to locate the plane after it lost contact, its wreckage was not discovered until March 25, 1969, near Anselmo, Nebraska.

January 12, 1938

U.S. secretary of the interior Harold Ickes issues an order that "surplus, opened lands of the Rosebud Indian Reservation…are hereby restored to tribal ownership for the use and benefit of the Rosebud Sioux Tribe of Indians of the Rosebud Indian Reservation."

January 13, 1893

The Western South Dakota Stockgrowers Association receives official documentation from the South Dakota secretary of state recognizing it as an incorporated entity. A small gathering, including notable cattlemen James "Scotty" Philip and Ed Lemmon, met the previous year in what became the first meeting of the Western South Dakota Stockgrowers Association. In 1937, the name changed to the South Dakota Stockgrowers Association.

January 14

1954

A wildcat discovery in Harding County leads to a well from which oil is extracted from a depth of over nine thousand feet. The well is labeled as a "wildcat" discovery, as there was no known potential for oil in the state prior to this. The well produced over 341,000 barrels of oil during its fifty years of operation.

2016

For the first time in South Dakota's legislative history, a "State of the Tribes" address is presented to a joint session of the South Dakota legislature. Harold Frazier, chair of the Cheyenne River Sioux Tribal Council, addressed the legislators on behalf of the nine federally recognized tribes in the state. According to Frazier, inadequate Indian Health Service care and the high rate of suicide among tribal youth are two of the biggest challenges facing tribes.

January 15, 1943

U.S. Marine Corps Reserve captain Joe Foss shoots down three more enemy planes, bringing his total to twenty-six Japanese planes in the last forty-four days. Foss's growing reputation as a World War II flying ace earned him a Congressional Medal of Honor, and his picture appeared on the cover of *Life* magazine. Foss later served as governor of South Dakota, the first president of the American Football League and president of the National Rifle Association.

January 16, 1900

The General Federation of Women's Clubs of South Dakota is organized. The South Dakota State Historical Society Archives holds the 1899–1958 records of the state organization, including the Pioneer Daughters Collection, which includes numerous accounts of early female pioneers and settlers from across the state.

January 17

1891

The dead from the December 29, 1890 Wounded Knee Massacre are buried in a mass grave. Retrieving the frozen bodies from across the countryside took several days.

2011

Approximately two hundred starlings are found mysteriously dead in Yankton. While some people initially believed that the birds were victims of cold weather, the U.S. Department of Agriculture accepted responsibility for the dead birds. According to the USDA, thousands of birds were defecating in the feed meal of a Nebraska feed lot about ten miles away. Due to the health hazard posed by the birds to livestock and farm workers, officials provided poisoned bait.

January 18, 1971

U.S. senator George McGovern gives an antiwar speech on television. McGovern made his opposition to the United States' involvement in Vietnam and Southeast Asia a major part of his 1972 campaign as the Democratic presidential candidate.

January 19, 1959

The McCarlson Waterfowl Production Area (WPA) in Day County, South Dakota, becomes the first to be purchased with Duck Stamp funds. According to the U.S. Fish and Wildlife Service, the purpose of the WPA program is to "preserve wetlands and grasslands critical to waterfowl and other wildlife." As public lands, the service oversees the management of the WPAs. As many as 95 percent of the WPAs are located in South Dakota, North Dakota, Minnesota and Montana, where an abundance of shallow wetlands, often referred to as prairie potholes, plays an important role for migratory waterfowl.

January 20, 1980

A DC-7 lands near Akaska with twenty-six thousand pounds of marijuana valued at $18 million, resulting in the largest drug bust in South Dakota history. Local ice fishermen spotted the plane as it was landing near the Missouri River and feared that it had mechanical problems. Authorities arrested six individuals, who were charged with being part of a drug-dealing operation based out of Colombia.

January 21, 1961

George McGovern officially assumes his role as the first director of the Food for Peace program, having been appointed by President John F. Kennedy. McGovern, who served two terms in the U.S. House of Representatives

(1957–61), lost his bid for the U.S. Senate in 1960, which made him available to become the Food for Peace program director.

January 22, 1943

The "world's greatest variance in temperature," according to the *Guinness Book of World Records*, occurs in Spearfish. Chinook winds created the greatest recorded temperature change in North America—the temperature went from minus four degrees Fahrenheit at 7:30 a.m. to forty-five degrees Fahrenheit, an increase of forty-nine degrees, in a two-minute time span.

January 23, 1964

South Dakota becomes the thirty-eighth state to ratify the Twenty-Fourth Amendment to the United States Constitution. The amendment abolished poll taxes. South Dakota's approval of the amendment meant that the required ratification by three-fourths of the state legislatures or state conventions was met; the Twenty-Fourth Amendment officially became part of the United States Constitution.

January 24, 1896

The Right Reverend Thomas O'Gorman is named bishop for the Catholic Diocese of Sioux Falls, which includes the region east of the Missouri River. O'Gorman became the second bishop of the diocese, following Bishop Martin Marty.

January 25, 1939

The U.S. Congress authorized the Badlands National Monument on March 4, 1929, the first day of Herbert Hoover's presidency. Although Congress had passed the authorization and President Calvin Coolidge had signed it on his last day in office, arrangements had to be made to acquire privately owned land for the national monument site. Almost a decade later, on January 25, 1939, President Franklin D. Roosevelt signed the proclamation making it the seventy-seventh monument within the National Park Service. In addition to its awe-inspiring scenery, Badlands National Park is known for having one of the world's richest deposits of fossils. Because a portion of the park is now included within the Pine Ridge Reservation, the Oglala Lakota Nation co-manages Badlands National Park with the U.S. National Park Service.

January 26, 1978

The National Park Service, under the Department of the Interior, adds Aberdeen's Wylie Park Pavilion to its National Register of Historic Places. Dating to around 1912, Wylie Park and the pavilion became a popular destination for many people, as it is today. When Aberdeen had streetcar service, many residents and visitors simply took advantage of the easy means of transportation to attend a variety of events hosted at the Pavilion. Among the many public events held at the pavilion were live music and dances and public and political speakers. And, yes, Lawrence Welk performed at the facility, too.

January 27, 1908

The first USS *South Dakota* is commissioned. From 1908 until 1920, the battleship went by the name USS *South Dakota*; from 1920 to 1927, it was named the USS *Huron*.

January 28, 2013

According to an Associated Press article, the South Dakota Animal Industry Board reported that there are several dozen South Dakotans who have licenses to possess exotic or "captive nondomestic" animals. The board's database shows that South Dakotans privately own animals including tigers, mountain lions, wolves, silver foxes, a leopard and a black bear.

January 29, 1917

Governor Peter Norbeck receives a letter of concern about the growing membership of the Non-Partisan League in South Dakota. The Non-Partisan League began in North Dakota with the intention of electing officials, regardless of political party affiliation, who opposed large corporations. Instead, the NPL advocated state-owned elevators, flour mills and other services vital to famers. Norbeck's friend B.B. Haugen noted that the "Non-Partisan crowd is coming down from the north like a swarm of grasshoppers." Norbeck, a progressive Republican who had been in office only a few weeks, sought to limit the Non-Partisan League's growing influence in the state.

January 30, 1901

The South Dakota Senate reports that it passed House Bill No. 10 the previous day. Having successfully passed both the House of Representatives and the Senate, Governor Charles Herreid signed the legislation on February 5, 1901. HB 10's wording stated that it was "A Bill for an Act establishing the Department of History of the State of South Dakota, and defining the powers and duties of the State Historical Society in connection therewith."

January 31, 1912

State Democrats meet in Pierre to discuss their support of a presidential candidate. Attendees spoke favorably of both Woodrow Wilson and Champ Clark as probable Democratic presidential candidates, but no official endorsement was made. Democrats, however, endorsed Richard Pettigrew for the U.S. Senate while supporting a national platform that included the initiative and referendum, the recall of judges and the direct election of U.S. senators.

February

February is the "Moon of the Dark Red Calves." It is a time when winter reaches its midpoint and the hope for warmer days and thaws increases. It is still a time, however, when low temperatures are common. Indeed, it is the month of the all-time lowest recorded temperature in the state's history. February marks the discovery of a lead plate indicating the white man's arrival to the state, and it marks the anniversary of a young basketball player whose death left a legacy that is still acknowledged annually.

February 1, 1911

South Dakota ratifies the Sixteenth Amendment of the U.S. Constitution, authorizing Congress to create a federal income tax. Congress proposed the amendment on July 12, 1909, and it was ratified on February 3, 1913. The concept of a national income tax had been one of the measures promoted by the Populist Party dating to the early 1890s.

February 2–3, 1912

Deadwood hosts the annual meeting of the South Dakota Good Roads Association. The morning session on the first day (February 2) involved preliminary business, as many of those attending from the eastern part of the state had not yet arrived due to their train being delayed. The afternoon featured automobile trips to experience firsthand the county highway improvements made between Deadwood and Spearfish and Deadwood and Pluma. The Saturday (February 3) session featured several relevant presentations on road and highway topics.

February 3, 1897

The state legislature passes legislation creating the South Dakota Board of Railroad Commissioners. The legislation gave the commissioners authority to set "reasonable maximum fares and charges for the transportation of passengers, freight, and cars on the railroads within the state." In addition, the maximum rate charged to passengers was not to exceed three cents per mile. The role of the Railroad Commissioners reflected the increasing resentment toward large railroad companies by members of the Populist Party.

February 4, 1890

The first South Dakota Supreme Court, comprising Justices Dighton Corson, A.G. Kellam and J.E. Bennett, convenes. The first session of the court took place in the Hughes County Courthouse, as the South Dakota State Capitol, a small wooden structure, only had room for the governor and the state legislature. Presiding judge Corson administered the oath to fifty-seven attorneys who were then officially permitted to appear before the state's supreme court.

February 5, 1901

The U.S. House of Representatives and Senate approve extending the timeline for the "commencement and completion of the bridge across the Missouri River at or near Oacoma, South Dakota." Due to the amended act, Congress set the new deadline for completion of the Chicago, Sioux Falls & Pacific Railway bridge to January 28, 1904. Congress initially passed the act authorizing the construction of the bridge on January 28, 1899, but construction was delayed, resulting in the extended completion deadline.

February 6, 1973

American Indian Movement activists arrive in Custer to protest State's Attorney Hobart Gates's decision to charge Darld Schmitz with manslaughter instead of murder in the case of Wesley Bad Heart Bull. The protesters numbered around two hundred and were led by well-known AIM leaders Russell Means and Dennis Banks. The protest turned into a riot, resulting in extensive property destruction at the courthouse and in the community. Both Means and Banks were among those later charged with rioting and assault. Means, an Oglala Lakota, received a thirty-day sentence along with a $100 fine plus court costs. Banks, who was not from South Dakota, fled the state after his conviction of rioting and assault. Nine years later, he turned himself in to state authorities.

February 7, 1908

President Theodore Roosevelt proclaims Jewel Cave a national monument. According to the National Park Service, Frank and Albert Michaud filed a mining claim at the site in 1900. When the Michaud brothers first discovered the cave, it was only a small hole with cold air blowing out of it. After they dynamited a larger entrance, they discovered that the cave included numerous calcite crystals that shimmered in the light, creating the appearance of jewels. The federal government eventually bought the mining claim with the cave entrance for approximately $750.

February 8, 1899

Due to threats to livestock, the state legislature passes "An Act to Encourage the Destruction of Coyotes, Wolves and Mountain Lions Within the State of South Dakota." A clause included in the law stated that "An emergency is hereby declared to exist, and this act shall take effect from and after its passage and approval." Specifically, individuals would receive the following bounties for animals killed within the state boundaries: coyotes, one dollar; wolves, three dollars; and mountain lions, three dollars.

February 9, 1992

Seventeen-year-old Pine Ridge High School basketball player SuAnne Big Crow dies in a car accident while on her way to the Hanson Anderson Miss Basketball banquet, where she was a finalist. A member of the Oglala Sioux Tribe, she was born and raised on the Pine Ridge Indian Reservation in southwestern South Dakota. The SuAnne Big Crow Boys and Girls Club in Pine Ridge, the first Boys and Girls Club to be established on an Indian reservation, serves as a reminder of how SuAnne wanted a "Happy Town" where Lakota children could learn, be safe and be happy. Since 1994, the "Spirit of Su" Award has been given to an outstanding senior female and male player at each state high school basketball tournament based on the criteria of outstanding athletic ability, leadership, character, sportsmanship and grade point average.

February 10, 1890

President Benjamin Harrison issues a proclamation supporting the March 2, 1890 Congressional legislation dividing a portion of the Great Sioux Reservation in South Dakota into separate reservations. As a result, the Great Sioux Reservation located throughout western South Dakota was divided into the Cheyenne River, Standing Rock, Lower Brulé, Pine Ridge and Rosebud Reservations. The 1868 Fort Laramie Treaty originally established the Great Sioux Reservation.

February 11, 1959

Standing Rock Sioux Tribe voters approve an amended constitution. Although the 1934 Indian Reorganization Act encouraged tribes to adopt democratic governments, the Standing Rock Sioux Tribe, which straddles the South Dakota–North Dakota border, already had provisions for a tribal council as early as 1914. As a result, the tribe differed from other area tribes by voting against the IRA.

February 12

1914

The *Turner County Herald* reports that James J. Hill has threatened to relocate the Great Northern Railroad division headquarters from Garretson to Jasper, Minnesota. The reason for Hill's threat was excessive drinking by railroad employees, which created problems for the railway company. Furthermore, Great Northern officials stated that no additional improvements would be made to railroad property in the community, which is in Minnehaha County, unless all of the saloons were closed. City officials took steps to curtail Hill's concerns, and the division headquarters remained in Garretson.

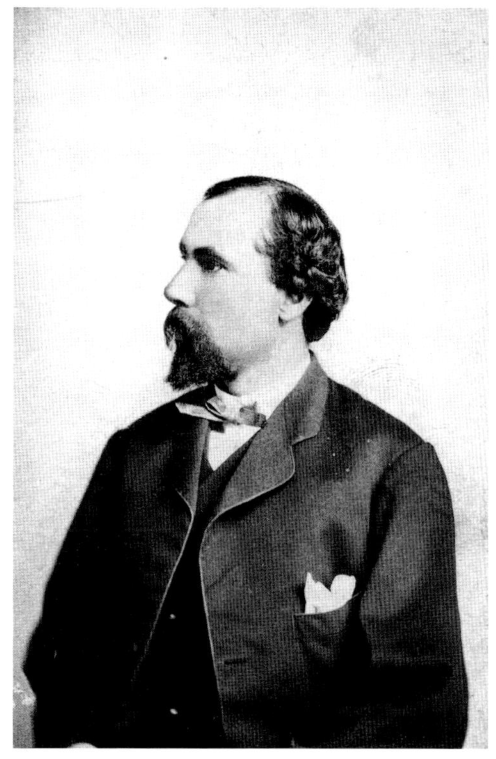

James Hill, Great Northern Railroad executive. *Minnesota Historical Society.*

2015

South Dakota Game, Fish and Parks officials release twenty-six bighorn sheep in Grizzly Gulch. Officials captured the bighorn sheep in Alberta, Canada, earlier in the week, and then they were trucked to Deadwood. The agreement between Canadian and state wildlife officials supported the reintroduction of bighorn sheep to the northern Black Hills after an absence of almost twenty-five years.

February 13, 1943

The Chinese ring-necked pheasant becomes the official state bird of South Dakota. In 1908, the first successful introduction of ring-necked pheasants took place near Doland in Spink County. In 1911, Game, Fish and Parks officials released approximately five hundred pheasants in Spink and Beadle Counties.

February 14, 1991

The South Dakota Lions Eye Bank officially opens in Sioux Falls after a successful fundraising campaign garnered over $70,000 through the work and contributions of the Lions, as well as other individual and group contributors. By the year's end, the Eye Bank placed ninety-nine corneas from 123 donors.

February 15, 1976

The State of South Dakota officially requests that California governor Edmund Gerald "Jerry" Brown Jr. extradite American Indian Movement leader Dennis Banks. Banks had been convicted for his role in a 1973 riot that took place in Custer. Banks eventually returned to South Dakota in 1984.

February 16, 1913

Schoolchildren discover a lead plate that had been left near the confluence of the Bad and Missouri Rivers on March 30, 1743, by François and Louis-Joseph Verendrye. This plate is the earliest evidence of white men in what is now South Dakota.

February 17, 1936

The temperature dropped to -58 Fahrenheit at McIntosh, setting the lowest recorded temperature for the state. Later, in July of the same year, the state's highest recorded temperature of 120 Fahrenheit was recorded—a range of 178 degrees from the coldest to the hottest recorded temperatures.

February 18, 1918

Throughout state history, the "Annual Report of the Railroad Commissioners of the State of South Dakota" often noted that one of the most common complaints filed with the Commission is the failure of companies to provide ample cars for transporting grain and livestock. In one case, the Railroad Commission's Annual Report shows that the Kimball State Bank filed a complaint on this date against the Chicago, Milwaukee & St. Paul Railway Company for "shortage of cars for shipment of stock." The company responded by providing the necessary cars, and officials closed the case on April 5, 1918.

February 19, 1913

South Dakota ratifies the Seventeenth Amendment, allowing for the direct election of U.S. senators. As with the Sixteenth Amendment, which created a federal income tax, the Populist Party of the 1890s supported the direct election of senators by each state's eligible voters. The Seventeenth Amendment was ratified on April 8, 1913, after having been approved by Connecticut.

February 20, 1892

The first Western South Dakota Stockgrowers Association meets at the Harney Hotel in Rapid City. The association can be traced back to territorial days when the Stockgrowers Association for the Territories of Dakota, Wyoming and Nebraska was founded in 1880. In 1937, a broader statewide membership led to the name being changed to the South Dakota Stockgrowers Association.

February 21, 1908

A political commentary in the *Dakota Farmers' Leader* newspaper from Canton targets U.S. senator Alfred Kittredge and his commitment to temperance. The unnamed writer stated that "Senator Kittredge on a recent visit to Hudson in this county patronized the saloons liberally and set 'em up for the boys like a brewer. Out at Plankinton he was seeking temperance bouquets from the W.C.T.U. [Woman's Christian Temperance Union] Such duplicity is disgusting."

February 22, 1889

Lame-duck president Grover Cleveland signs the Enabling Act of 1889. The act enabled the creation of four new states: South Dakota, North Dakota, Montana and Washington. On November 2 of that year President Benjamin Harrison signed the documents officially admitting the "twin" states of North Dakota and South Dakota into the Union as the thirty-ninth and fortieth states, respectively.

February 23, 1978

The honey bee "is hereby designated as the official insect of the State of South Dakota." South Dakota is a leader in honey production. Since the honey bee plays an important role in South Dakota agriculture, it is considered essential to the state's economy.

February 24, 1954

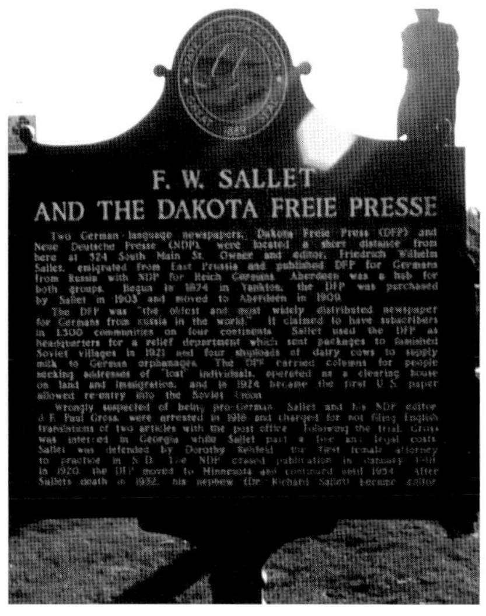

Dakota Freie Presse/F.W. Sallet historical marker. *Brad Tennant.*

The German-language newspaper *Dakota Freie Presse* ceases publication. It began in 1874 in Yankton, Dakota Territory, and became the most widely distributed newspaper for Germans from Russia. F.W. Sallet purchased and moved the paper to Aberdeen in 1909. As editor of both the *Dakota Freie Presse* and the *Neue Deutsche Presse*, Sallet came under a great deal of scrutiny with the increasingly anti-German sentiment that resulted largely from the outbreak of World War I. Publishing of the *Neue Deutsche Presse* ended in early 1918, and the *Dakota Freie Presse* relocated to Minnesota in 1920, where it remained until its end in 1954.

February 25, 1992

South Dakota holds its primary elections for president. Democratic voters chose Senator Bob Kerrey of Nebraska, who received slightly more than 40 percent of the Democratic vote. On the Republican side, over 69 percent of the voters supported incumbent George H.W. Bush, with the remaining delegates being "unpledged" for the Republican National Convention. In the November national election, Bush received the state's three electoral votes, although Arkansas governor Bill Clinton, the Democratic Party's nominee, won the presidential election.

February 26, 1947

Governor George T. Mickelson signs into law the Electric Cooperative Act, which permitted the organization of nonprofit electric cooperatives throughout the state. This legislation became instrumental in promoting and increasing rural electrification.

February 27, 1973

American Indian Movement (AIM) members begin a seventy-one-day occupation of Wounded Knee on the Pine Ridge Indian Reservation. The occupation focused on bringing attention to concerns regarding American Indian issues, including the federal government's failure to abide by past treaty agreements. Although many non-Indians sympathized with those who occupied the community, the tribal government and many Oglala Lakota opposed the measures used by AIM.

February 28, 2003

South Dakota officially adopts rodeo as its state sport. Many of the events associated with rodeo emerged from ranchers and hired hands working with horses and cattle long before South Dakota became a state. Over the years, events became more organized, and competitive rodeos became commonplace. Rosebud is believed to have hosted the first organized rodeo in South Dakota, in the late 1890s.

February 29, 1940

A special ceremony at Berkeley, California, honors Ernest O. Lawrence, who becomes the first native of South Dakota to become a Nobel laureate. He received the 1939 Noble Prize in physics. The outbreak of World War II caused his award ceremony to be moved to California. Born in Canton, Lawrence received his doctorate from Yale University and had an illustrious career at the University of California–Berkeley. Dr. Lawrence received his Noble Prize in the field of accelerator physics and was specifically cited by the Nobel Committee "for the invention and development of the cyclotron and for results obtained with it, especially with regard to artificial radioactive elements." During World War II, Lawrence became a major contributor to the Manhattan Project. He later became an advocate for an international agreement to end atomic bomb testing. On the Periodic Table, the chemical element Lawrencium (Lr) is named in his honor.

March

March is a time when late winter or early spring weather can still be treacherous. It is a month that includes an accident that led to the "Spirit of Six" award, a bank robbery and the beginning of a televised children's program that aired for over forty years. March is the month that can aptly be called the "Moon of the Snowblind."

March 1, 1900

The South Dakota School for the Blind officially opens in Gary. Community members actively sought to have Gary become the home of the South Dakota "Blind Asylum." When the Board of Charities and Corrections visited the town, it determined that additional facilities were needed. Consequently, when the official opening of the school occurred, it included the former county courthouse plus a new two-story building. The School for the Blind remained in Gary until the 1959 state legislature approved moving it to Aberdeen. Classes at the Aberdeen campus began in September 1961.

March 2–4, 1966

One of the most severe blizzards in South Dakota history began on Tuesday, March 2, and continued for the next two days. The three-day storm included freezing drizzle, heavy snowfall, high winds and low temperatures—all characteristic of any blizzard. However, the storm is especially noted for its consequences. Since spring-like weather was becoming more common, many people simply were not prepared for the early March storm system that wreaked havoc throughout much of the state. Six deaths were attributed to the blizzard, and thousands of livestock were lost. In addition to the harsh weather conditions, many ranchers were already experiencing calving and lambing, and many of the young animals simply could not survive under such conditions. In the western part of the state, estimates placed the number of cattle and sheep killed somewhere between forty thousand and sixty thousand head.

March 3, 1925

The U.S. Congress passes legislation approving the carving of Mount Rushmore and authorizing "the establishment of a memorial commemorative of our national history and progress."

March 4, 1929

President Calvin Coolidge signs Public Law No. 1021, authorizing the Badlands National Monument, on his last day in office. The U.S. House of Representatives and the U.S. Senate had passed the legislation two days earlier. Although the Badlands National Monument was authorized on this date, the legislation first called for privately owned land within the proposed monument boundary to be purchased. As a result, it was not officially established until President Franklin D. Roosevelt signed the authorization in 1939. In 1978, the name officially changed to Badlands National Park.

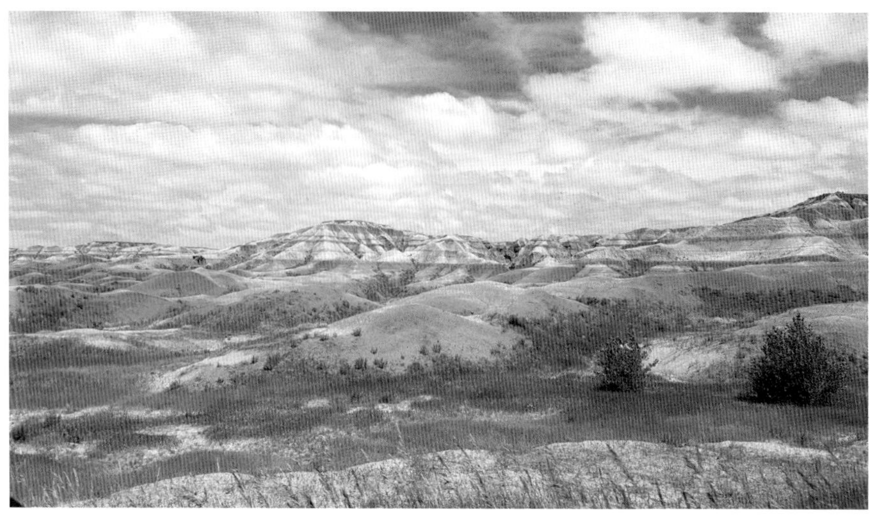

The South Dakota Badlands. *Jaret Copeman/Sydney Johnson.*

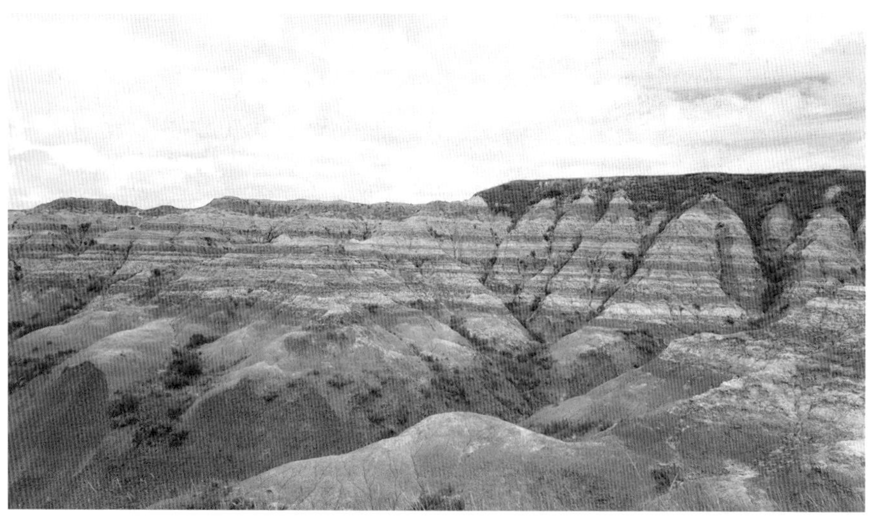

Above: Badlands. *Jaret Copeman/Sydney Johnson.*

Opposite: Badlands. *Jaret Copeman/Sydney Johnson.*

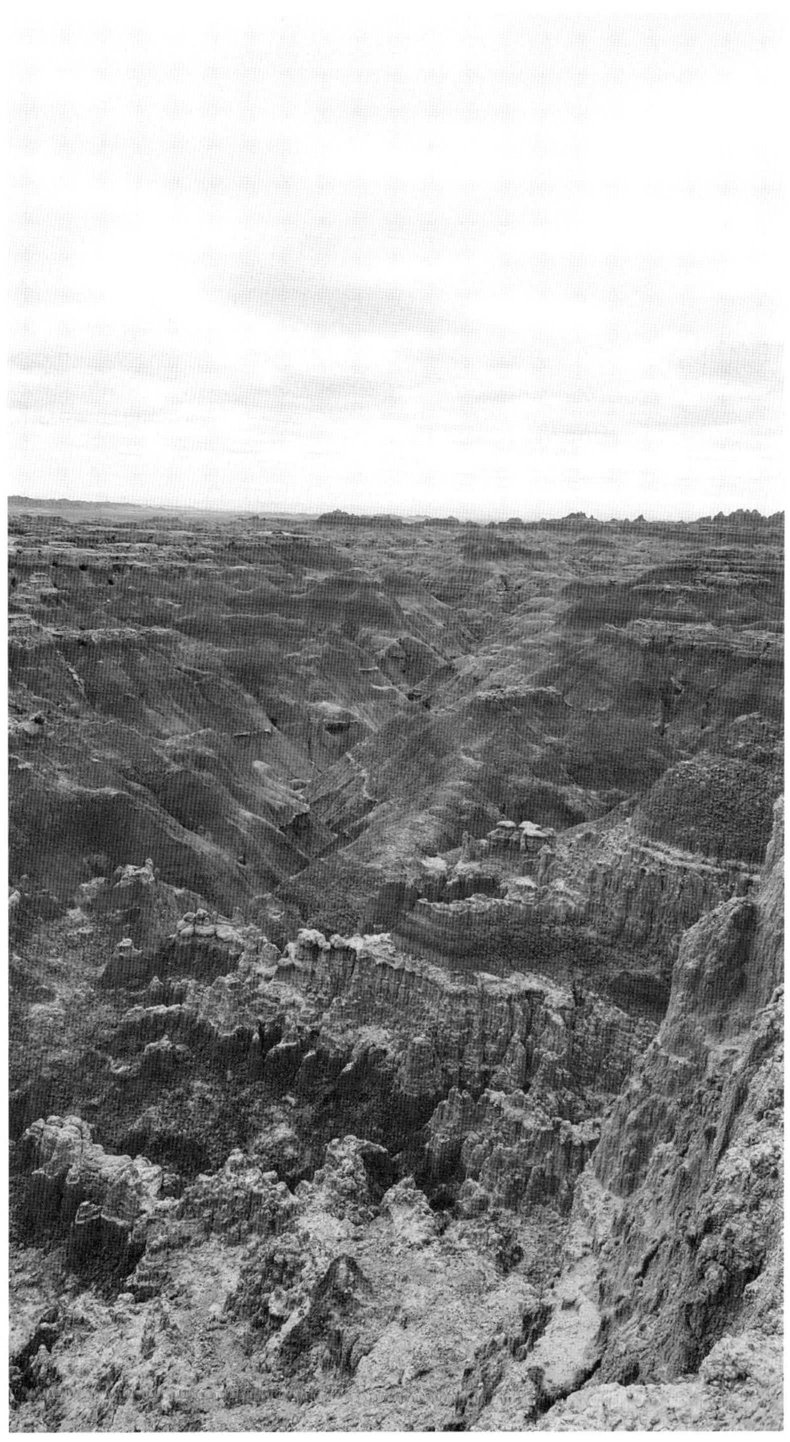

March 5, 1949

Governor George T. Mickelson signs legislation designating the coyote as South Dakota's official state animal. The animal was chosen for this designation, despite having been actively hunted since territorial days.

March 6, 1934

Infamous bank robbers John Dillinger and Baby Face Nelson rob the Security National Bank and Trust in Sioux Falls. Dillinger, Nelson and their gang took four female bank tellers hostage during their getaway. The women were later released. Officials never recovered the approximately $46,000 said to have been stolen.

March 7, 1955

KELO-TV weatherman Dave Dedrick dons a blue uniform as "Captain 11" for a children's televised afterschool program. After a run of forty-one years, KELO televised the last Captain 11 program on December 28, 1996.

March 8, 1909

The original design of the state flag is adopted. State senator Ernest May originally proposed the notion of a flag to Doane Robinson, the director of the State Historical Society. Robinson then arranged for Ida Anding, a legislative librarian, to design the flag. According to the South Dakota Bureau of Administration, Anding's design included the following description until 1963:

> *The Flag of South Dakota shall consist of a field of blue, one and two-thirds as long as it is wide, in the center of which shall be a blazing sun in gold, two-fifths as wide in diameter as the width of the flag. Above this sun shall be arranged in the arc of the circle, in gold letters, the words "South Dakota"*

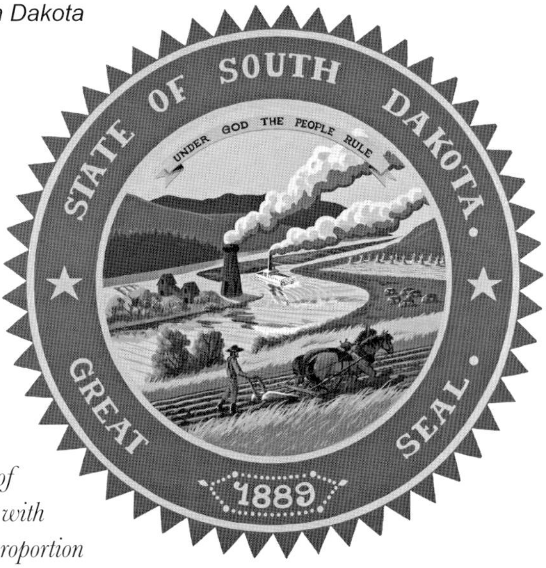

South Dakota state seal. *South Dakota Secretary of State.*

> *and below this sun in the arc of the circle shall be arranged the words in gold letters, "The Sunshine State," and on the reverse of the blazing sun shall be printed in dark blue the Great Seal of the State Of South Dakota. The edges of the flag shall be trimmed with a fringe of gold, to be in proportion to the width of the flag. The staff shall be surmounted by a spearhead to which shall be attached cord and tassels of suitable length and size.*

As a cost-saving measure in 1963, the state seal was integrated onto the same side as the sun. In 1992, "The Mount Rushmore State" replaced "The Sunshine State" as the official state nickname. In 2015, a former employee of the South Dakota Secretary of State's office stole an original flag, which was later recovered.

March 9, 1987

Former governor Richard Kneip passes away. Kneip became South Dakota's twenty-fifth governor in 1970 at the age of thirty-seven, making him the youngest governor in state history. In addition, he also became the first Roman Catholic to serve as the state's governor. When he was elected in 1970, the term of office was two years. Kneip won reelection in 1972; then, due to a constitutional change, voters reelected him again in 1974 for a four-year term. This meant that Kneip became the only person to be elected for three consecutive terms. Such a feat can no longer be achieved with the current state constitution. Near the end of his third term, Kneip resigned as governor to become U.S. ambassador to Singapore during the Jimmy Carter administration.

March 10, 1905

The South Dakota legislature approves an act amending the qualifications for lower-grade teacher certifications. According to the act, applicants for teaching certificates "shall pass an examination in orthography, reading, writing, arithmetic, geography, physical geography, English grammar, physiology and hygiene, history of the United States, civil government, current events, American literature, South Dakota history, drawing and didactics."

March 11, 1949

In accordance with the Indian Reorganization Act of 1934, the Crow Creek Sioux Tribe approves its constitution and bylaws by a vote of 168 to 76. President Abraham Lincoln's administration established the Crow Creek Indian Reservation after the 1862 Minnesota Uprising as a place to relocate Dakota Indians from Minnesota into Dakota Territory. The Indian Reorganization Act reversed several decades of federal assimilation policy designed to erode tribal influences.

March 12, 1952

South Dakotans who happen to be in the District of Columbia on March 17, 1952, are invited to a St. Patrick's Day reception and dance to be held at the Washington National Airport. The South Dakota State Society of Washington, D.C. is hosting the event, and Senator Karl Mundt, who serves as the society's president, encourages all South Dakotans who will be in the area to attend.

March 13, 2015

Having passed both houses of the state legislature, Senate Bill 86 is signed into law. It sets the term of the South Dakota Poet Laureate to four years. "Badger" Clark became the state's first poet laureate in 1937. In September 2014, poet laureate David Allan Evans resigned after having held the appointment since 2002. Evans, who was only the third person to be designated poet laureate, stated that he believed other poets in the state should be allowed an opportunity to be appointed.

March 14

1951

While some cast the blame for the country's rapidly increasing living costs on American farmers, U.S. senator Karl Mundt defends farmers in his weekly report. According to Mundt, "by comparison with prevailing wages and profits the farmer's net income is lower than in 1947, 1948, or 1949."

1973

Lead, South Dakota, sets a state record for the most snowfall within a twenty-four-hour period, when fifty-two inches is recorded on this date.

March 15, 1954

On a signal from President Dwight Eisenhower in the White House, Governor Sigurd Anderson throws the switch for the first power unit of the Fort Randall Dam. Authorized by the Flood Control Act of 1944, construction of the dam began in 1946. The Fort Randall Dam, which is located on the Missouri River in the south-central part of South Dakota, created Lake Francis Case.

March 16, 1992

The South Dakota Air National Guard's 114th Tactical Fighter Group unit is renamed the 114th Fighter Group. In June 1992, it became part of the new Air Combat Command. In October 1995, the 114th Fighter Group was re-designated again as the 114th Fighter Wing. According to its website, 114th Fighter Wing's mission is "To provide combat capable aircraft, air crew, support personnel, and equipment to augment existing active forces during times of crisis, national emergencies or war; To provide personnel and resources to protect life and property, and to preserve peace, order and public safety in the State of South Dakota; [and] To participate in local, state, and national programs that add value to the communities of America."

March 17, 1968

Six Rapid City Cobbler cheerleaders are among nine individuals who die in a plane crash as they are returning from the State A Boys Basketball Tournament in Sioux Falls. Beginning in 1970, the South Dakota Peace Officers' Association began presenting a trophy to the outstanding cheerleaders of the state basketball tournaments. Today, the Spirit of Six award is presented to the outstanding basketball cheerleaders at the AA, A and B boys' and girls' tournaments.

March 18, 2013

A federal grand jury issues a subpoena to the South Dakota state government as part of its investigation into Joop Bollen and the federal government's Immigrant Investor Program, commonly referred to as the EB-5 Program. According to a Sioux Falls *Argus Leader* article, the "'EB-5' is a complex affair at the intersection of government, business, crime and politics in South Dakota."

March 19, 1934

Andrew Lee, who served as the third governor of South Dakota, passes away at his Vermillion home, one day after his eighty-seventh birthday. Voters elected Lee to the governor's office in 1896 as a Populist candidate and again in 1898 as a Fusionist candidate with support from an alliance of Populists, Democrats and Free Silver Republicans.

March 20, 1918

The South Dakota legislature ratifies the proposed Eighteenth Amendment to the U.S. Constitution prohibiting "the manufacture, sale, or transportation of intoxicating liquors." When South Dakota became a state in 1889, voters had already approved of prohibition in the state constitution. It was removed in 1896, but the state legislature continued to address the issue of restricting alcohol throughout the years until the Eighteenth Amendment was ratified in 1919.

March 21, 1998

A landslide affects the Homestake Mining Company's Open Cut surface mining operations at Lead. Mining activities temporarily ceased and were resumed a few weeks later.

March 22, 1999

The Sioux Falls Weather Forecast Office, under the National Oceanic and Atmospheric Administration, upgrades its computer system to the Advanced Weather Interactive Processing System (AWIPS). The new technology allows the forecast office to make significant improvements in its weather forecasts.

March 23, 2003

The 109th Engineering Battalion, based out of Sturgis, becomes the first unit of the South Dakota National Guard to enter Iraq as part of Operation Iraqi Freedom.

March 24, 1973

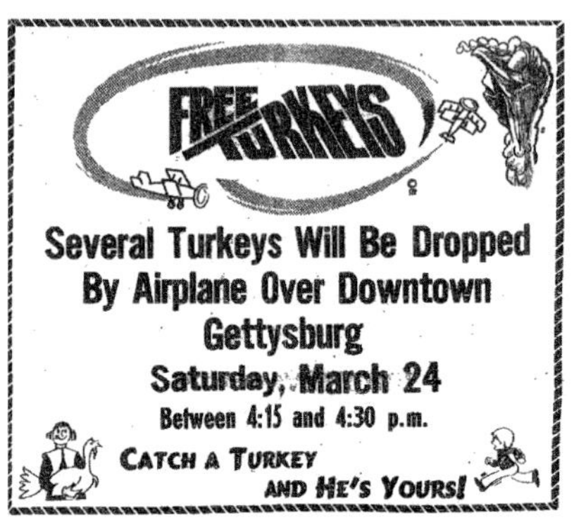

Newspaper advertisement for Turkey Drop. *From the* Potter County News.

As part of a Farmers Day appreciation, sponsors in Gettysburg drop several live turkeys from an airplane with the promotional slogan of "Catch a Turkey and He's Yours!" An editorial column in the *Potter County News* stated afterward that "at 75 miles or so an hour, before the first turkey could get oriented he had already hit ground—No flying, no gliding, just thud." A total of six turkeys were dropped. Two hit power lines, two landed on roofs and the remaining two landed near Main Street.

March 25, 1989

A questionnaire is mailed to 286 South Dakota elementary school principals as part of a study conducted by the University of South Dakota's School of Education. A total of 164 questionnaires was returned and used as the data for the study titled "Status of Social Studies Education in South Dakota Elementary Schools." According to the study's recommendations, "elementary schools in South Dakota should rely less on a textbook dominated social studies curriculum and use a greater variety of instructional materials and strategies." In addition, more emphasis should be placed on "experiential learning that encourages critical thinking and application," and more time "must be devoted to social studies instruction at all grade levels."

March 26, 2007

A South Dakota House of Representatives resolution recognizes William Farber, honoring his "life, achievements, and indomitable spirit." Farber, who passed away two days before the legislative resolution, had an illustrious career as a political science professor at the University of South Dakota, and he is credited with being the founder of the South Dakota Legislative Research Council.

March 27, 2011

The Thirty-Fourth Bomber Squadron, known as the Thunderbirds, becomes the first B-1 combat mission to fly from the United States with the objective of striking overseas targets. The Thirty-Fourth Bomber Squadron flew nonstop from the Ellsworth Air Force Base to Libya as part of Operation Odyssey Dawn.

March 28, 1964

Southwestern South Dakota experiences tremors from an earthquake that had its epicenter near Merriman, Nebraska. The strongest tremor measured 5.1 on the Richter scale. Reports of minor damage, including cracks to wall and ceiling plaster and some broken glass, came from several communities and farms. Four days earlier, on March 24, people at Wind Cave National Park experienced trembling that lasted for only a few seconds. Officials placed the epicenter near Van Tassell, Wyoming.

March 29, 1899

The First South Dakota Regiment encounters a serious exchange of fire from Filipinos near the Guiguinto River during what became known as the Philippine Insurrection. Ten soldiers of the First Regiment suffered wounds from the day's battle.

March 30, 2009

Governor Michael Rounds signs legislation that "prohibits smoking or carrying of any lighted tobacco product in public places or places of employment." The state senate had passed the smoking ban on March 4, and the state House of Representatives had passed it on March 9.

March 31, 1946

After serving pheasant sandwiches to thousands of military personnel, the Aberdeen Railway Station Canteen discontinues serving meals. The canteen started serving meals to troops in August 1943 as they traveled through Aberdeen by passenger train.

April

Despite Black Elk's reference to April being the "Moon of the Red Grass Appearing," April showers were not always the case. During the Dirty Thirties, a massive black blizzard occurred during the springtime due to the extreme drought conditions. April will be noted as the month in which the state lost one of its most beloved governors. It is also a month when members of the Cheyenne River Sioux Tribe were recognized for making the ultimate sacrifice during World War I.

April 1

1962

Flooding causes portions of the Interstate 29 bridge from Iowa to South Dakota to collapse. Construction of the bridge over the Big Sioux River had been completed the previous September. The South Dakota Highway Commission called for an investigation into the collapse, but preliminary accounts stated that rapid water movement likely weakened the footings of the bridge.

1998

U.S. representative John Thune speaks favorably of HR 2400, the Building Efficient Surface Transportation Equity Act of 1998. Noting that South Dakota's state highway system includes over 7,800 miles of roads, Thune specifically mentioned his amendment to the bill, which allows federal bridge funding to be used for a de-icer developed in conjunction with the South Dakota Department of Transportation, the South Dakota School of Mines and Technology and private enterprise. In his speech, Thune lauded the de-icer, known as sodium acetate/formate, as "a cost-effective, environmentally sound way to keep bridges clear of dangerous icing conditions."

April 2, 1987

The bill authorizing the South Dakota Lottery is signed. In the November 1986 election, 60 percent of the state's voters approved amending the South Dakota constitution to allow the state lottery. The first scratch ticket was sold about six months later, on September 30, 1987.

April 3, 1926

The first state poet laureate, Badger Clark, shares his work at the first cowboy poetry event in Elko, Nevada. One of his most well-known works, "A Cowboy's Prayer," has been widely circulated over the years; unfortunately, it is often cited as either "author unknown" or "anonymous." The South Dakota Historical Society Foundation continues to reprint Clark's published works as well as other materials about Badger Clark.

April 4, 1936

The Flandreau Santee Sioux Tribe overwhelmingly approves its constitution by a vote of eighty-three to six. As he did with other tribes throughout the country, the secretary of the interior, Harold Ickes, also recommended approval of the Flandreau Santee Sioux Tribe's constitution and bylaws as required by the 1934 Indian Reorganization Act.

April 5–6, 1903

President Theodore Roosevelt arrives in Sioux Falls for what would be his first stop in a tour of twelve eastern South Dakota communities to give his speech regarding the country's prosperity. He states that "there can be no real general prosperity unless based on the foundation of the prosperity of the wage-worker and the tiller of the soil." Traveling by train, Roosevelt, following his appearance in Sioux Falls, made stops in Lennox, Yankton, Scotland, Tripp, Parkston, Mitchell, Woonsocket, Alpena, Tulare, Redfield and Aberdeen.

April 7, 1991

Upon reporting for work at a convenience store in Dallas, South Dakota, Ionia Klein finds an unclaimed lottery ticket with winning numbers worth $12.5 million. When the ticket was printed the previous day, the customer said that he wanted five $1 tickets, not one $5 ticket, so the ticket was not sold. Klein then bought the ticket when she discovered the winning numbers and signed her name. The store owners, however, also filed a claim, stating that since the ticket had been discarded, they should be the rightful winners. In the end, media reports stated that Klein and the store owners split the amount, with Klein receiving 42 percent and the store owners receiving 58 percent.

April 8

1947

George Sitts, thirty-three, becomes the only person to be executed in South Dakota by the electric chair. Sitts shot and killed a liquor store clerk in Minnesota and later two law enforcement officials. Sitts became the fourth person to be sentenced to death by the electric chair since it was first authorized in 1939; however, the first three convicted murderers received commuted sentences of life imprisonment. A large gathering of forty-one witnesses watched as Sitts received four successive electric shocks.

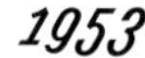

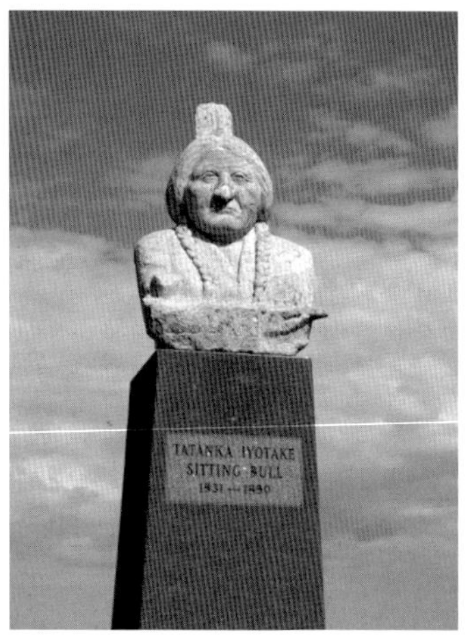

A group of Mobridge men secretly exhume the remains of Sitting Bull from his burial site near Fort Yates, North Dakota, and re-bury the bones at a site overlooking the Missouri River across from Mobridge. The businessmen hoped that Sitting Bull's new grave site would attract tourists to the area. As a precaution to prevent any future grave robbing, the group covered the remains with concrete.

Sitting Bull Memorial. *Brigid Tennant.*

April 9, 1988

A federal district court jury awards the State of South Dakota approximately $600 million as the result of an antitrust lawsuit against Kansas City Southern Railways. The antitrust case focused on Kansas City Southern Railways' efforts with other railroad companies to stop Energy Transportation Systems, Inc. (ETSI) from purchasing Missouri River water from the state. The water was to be used in a coal slurry pipeline that would transport crushed coal from Wyoming to southern states.

April 10, 2006

The Corson County Courthouse is the victim of arson. A county employee later admitted that he started the fire that destroyed the courthouse in McIntosh. The courthouse, a wooden structure built in 1910, was the last wood-frame building in the state still being used as a courthouse.

April 11, 1892

President Benjamin Harrison issues an official proclamation that the Lake Traverse Reservation of the Sisseton-Wahpeton Dakota Indians, having been subjected to conditions of the Allotment Act, shall be opened to settlement under the terms of the act of Congress approved on March 3, 1891. Non-Indian settlement was to begin no sooner than noon on April 15, 1892.

April 12, 1892

The Meade County Commission decides to discontinue bounties on wolves. According to information provided by Meade County, the county commission passed a resolution explaining that "there was no money in the General Fund…to pay the bounty on wolf scalps."

April 13, 1950

A press release from the U.S. Fish and Wildlife Service announces that funding is again available to plant shelterbelts to provide cover for pheasants during the winter months. The shelterbelt program was one of the conservation programs created under the 1937 Pittman-Robertson Federal Aid to Wildlife program. The 1950 shelterbelt program included planting trees such as "Russian olive, wild plum, sandcherry, Chinese elm, green ash, and boxelder." In addition to the benefits to the pheasant population, the U.S. Fish and Wildlife Service and the Department of the Interior support planting shelterbelts as a soil conservation measure.

April 14, 1935

One of the worst dust storms in South Dakota history occurs. The drought of the 1930s left little vegetation to hold the topsoil down. As a result, the strong winds common to the plains created dust clouds that blew for miles. Given the severity of the dust storms on this particular day, it soon became commonly known as "Black Sunday."

April 15, 1892

The Lake Traverse Reservation, home to the Sisseton-Wahpeton Oyate, is opened to non-Indian settlers seeking land. The reservation became the first in the state to be subjected to the allotment process, which created surplus lands for white settlers. Due to the considerable number of settlers who took advantage of the reservation's opening, it is often noted as the largest land rush in state history.

April 16, 1976

The state mourns the passing of Vera Bushfield. She served as the state's First Lady when her husband, Harlan Bushfield, served as governor from 1939 to 1943. After his term as governor, state voters elected Harlan to the U.S. Senate, where he served from 1943 until his passing in September 1948. Governor George T. Mickelson then appointed Vera as her husband's replacement in the Senate, a position she held from October 6 to December 26, 1948, when she resigned. Upon her resignation, Governor Mickelson then appointed the newly elected Karl Mundt to the U.S. Senate, which allowed him to have slightly more seniority than other senators who had been elected in 1948.

April 17, 1989

The Bureau of Land Management issues a two-page report concerning the oil and gas potential in Corson County. The narrative stated that Corson

County, like neighboring Perkins County, has a "moderate development potential" and that exploratory wells will determine the likelihood of future oil well drilling in the county.

April 18, 2011

A South Dakota Housing Development Authority press release states that, effective this day, the price of a Governor's House is $35,500, an increase of $2,500. The SDHDA oversees the Governor's House Program, in which inmates at the Mike Durfee State Prison in Springfield construct affordable houses for families with limited incomes.

April 19, 1993

Governor George S. Mickelson and seven other men die in a plane crash near Dubuque, Iowa. Mickelson, fifty-two, was serving his second term as governor, having been elected in 1986 and then reelected in 1990. His father, George T. Mickelson, also served as governor—George T. and George S. Mickelson were the only father and son to serve as the state's governors.

April 20, 1904

General S.J. Conklin, who served as the first adjutant general of South Dakota's National Guard, lists a number of uniform expenses in his "Report of the Adjutant General." Itemized expenses for the state militia on this date included a variety of officer uniforms, listed at ten dollars each.

April 21, 1948

Pierre hosts a Women's Day Rededication Program, which included a play, *A Pageant of Local History*, that portrayed a variety of historic events. In addition, Pierre hosted a traveling exhibit featuring more than one hundred documents significant to the nation's heritage.

April 22, 2011

On the thirty-first anniversary of Earth Day, financial news company 24/7 Wall St. lists South Dakota as the sixth-greenest state in the country. 24/7 Wall St. noted that the state "only had 14 EPA violations since 2000, far and away the fewest in the nation."

April 23, 1890

Suffragette Susan B. Anthony arrives in South Dakota. Representing the National American Woman Suffrage Association, Anthony attended more than twenty meetings in communities throughout the eastern part of the state.

April 24, 2008

The Journey North Monarch Butterfly migration report includes an early spring sighting of a monarch butterfly in Sioux Falls. The sighting was reported by a reliable observer, who realized that the larger migration of monarchs from Mexico was still several hundred miles to the south.

April 25–26, 1899

On April 25, two members of the First South Dakota Volunteer Infantry, Company B, are reported as "wounded in action" while serving in the Philippines. In addition, a Company B soldier died of disease that same day, while another was "killed in action" the following day.

April 27, 2005

After receiving input from citizens around the state, Governor M. Michael Rounds recommends the images to appear on the state's commemorative quarter. His recommendation is that the faces of Mount Rushmore appear on one side and a pheasant, the official state bird, on the other.

April 28, 1902

Fire destroys the Aberdeen Grain Palace, which was constructed in 1893. The palace featured annual fall designs made from local grains and grasses. On October 14, 1899, President William McKinley addressed a large crowd as part of the welcome home celebration for members of the First Regiment South Dakota Volunteers after their return from service in the Spanish-American War. On July 4, 1901, the funeral service for Senator James Kyle, who is credited with legislation establishing Labor Day, was held at the Grain Palace.

April 29, 1930

Congress passes an act "in honor of deceased chiefs of the Cheyenne River Sioux Tribe of Indians and the valiant men of that tribe who made the Supreme Sacrifice in the service of the United States in the World War, 1917–1918." A memorial with twenty-five names is located in Eagle Butte.

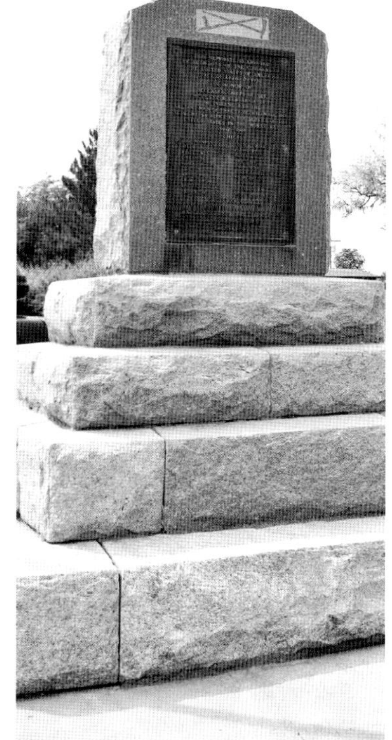

Cheyenne River Sioux Tribe World War I Memorial. *Brad Tennant.*

April 30, 1898

The payroll for the South Dakota Reform School in Plankinton shows monthly wages ranging from $5 to $200. Descriptions of work roles included supervisors, farmhands, teachers, food service workers and the superintendent, C.W. Ainsworth, and his wife. Together, the Ainsworths received a total of $200 per month.

May

The springtime weather has its extremes. Although temperatures increase, the weather can still vary, from late-season blizzards to heavy rainfall and tornadoes. May includes stories of a runaway elephant, dinosaurs, a teenager beginning a flight around the world and the dedication of one of the state's most beautiful churches. May is the "Moon When the Ponies Shed."

May 1, 2015

Shannon County is officially renamed Oglala Lakota County. In a November 2014 referendum, 80 percent of the county's voters approved the name change. As a formality, the South Dakota legislature passed House Joint Resolution 1005, and Governor Dennis Daugaard signed the proclamation noting the change on April 1, 2015. The name "Oglala Lakota County" then went into effect one month after Governor Daugaard's proclamation. The county had been named for Peter Shannon, chief justice of the Dakota Territorial Supreme Court. The name change aptly reflects that most of the county's residents are members of the Oglala Sioux Tribe.

May 2, 2006

According to the Centers for Disease Control, South Dakota is one of eleven states collectively reporting 2,597 cases of mumps from the first of the year through May 2.

May 3–4, 1905

The National Weather Service lists the spring blizzard of May 3–4 as the worst late-season blizzard in the state's short history. Livestock herds in western South Dakota were hit especially hard. Some ranchers reported losses as high as 90 percent of their herds.

May 5, 2007

The National Weather Service confirms that twenty-five tornadoes made ground contact in the southeastern part of the state within a six-hour period.

May 6, 2007

Spring showers set a state record for precipitation in a twenty-four-hour period. On this day in South Dakota history, Groton received 8.74 inches of rain.

May 7, 2015

Community members vote to make the Buffalo Chip campground and concert venue an incorporated town. Although the vote was forty-three to zero, a judge later nullified the action, based on several irregularities, including the residency of some who voted.

May 8

1965

An F5 tornado develops in Tripp County, and an F3 or F4 tornado destroys a Gregory County farm.

1973

The Wounded Knee occupation ends after seventy-one days. American Indian Movement (AIM) members began the occupation in February as a means to bring attention to concerns regarding American Indian issues, including the federal government's failure to abide by past treaty agreements.

2015

President Barack Obama gives the commencement address at Lake Area Technical Institute in Watertown. Obama's visit to South Dakota made him the fourth president to visit all fifty states, joining former presidents Richard Nixon, Bill Clinton and George H.W. Bush in doing so.

May 9

1900

Sioux Falls hosts the Populist Party's national presidential convention. Convention delegates endorsed William Jennings Bryan for president. Although supported by the Populist Party, Bryan ran as a Democrat.

1922

WCAT, or Wildcat Radio, becomes the first licensed radio station in the state. A group of electrical engineering students at South Dakota School of Mines and Technology established the station and began by broadcasting weather and news information. Music and sports broadcasts were added later. WCAT operated from 1922 to 1952, when larger commercial stations proved to be too much competition.

May 10, 2015

The community of Delmont suffers severe EF2 tornado damage, but fortunately, there are no deaths.

May 11, 1896

The *Chicago Tribune* publishes a news article out of Pierre regarding the growing discontent toward the state constitutional provision prohibiting the manufacture and sale of intoxicating liquor. Voters approved prohibition 40,234 to 34,510 in the state's first election in 1889; however, voters successfully repealed prohibition in the 1896 election by a vote of 31,901 to 24,901.

May 12, 1984

The University of South Dakota–Springfield conducts its last commencement. Governor William Janklow and the South Dakota state legislature decided to close the college and turn it into a medium-security prison. Today, the campus is home to the Mike Durfee State Prison.

May 13, 1904

President Theodore Roosevelt proclaims that all lands ceded by the Sioux Tribe of the Rosebud Reservation be opened to non-Indian settlement under the general provisions of the homestead and town site laws of the United States beginning at 9:00 a.m. on the eighth day of August 1904.

Exceptions included land to be used for educational purposes and land reserved for the American Missionary Society and the Roman Catholic Church for mission purposes.

May 14, 1916

A five-ton circus elephant becomes uncontrollable in Elkton. The elephant, named Hero, began destroying circus property and put his keeper in mortal danger. After escaping, townspeople pursued him. Hero was shot numerous times over a twelve-hour period, and he died from his wounds.

May 15, 1919

After a committee of South Dakota veterans attends the first national meeting to organize the American Legion, promoters create a provisional South Dakota American Legion at Vermillion, with Theodore Johnson of Sioux Falls as chair.

May 16, 1895

President Grover Cleveland issues a proclamation stating that the lands acquired from the Yankton Tribe of Sioux, or "Dacotah Indians," will be opened to settlement beginning at noon on the twenty-first day of May 1895.

May 17, 1916

A hearing is held in Onaka as the result of a complaint filed against the Minneapolis & St. Louis Railway Company regarding the company's decision to discontinue passenger service on the LeBeau Branch. Officials of the Minneapolis & St. Louis later reversed their decision and re-established the passenger service.

May 18

1933

Camp Este, the state's first Civilian Conservation Corps camp, is established. The CCC, a major part of Franklin D. Roosevelt's New Deal program, emphasized itself as a work relief program for unemployed, single men. Camp Este, also referred to as Nemo, oversaw the thinning of trees, road construction, trail maintenance and a variety of other conservation-minded projects. Camp Este closed in July 1942.

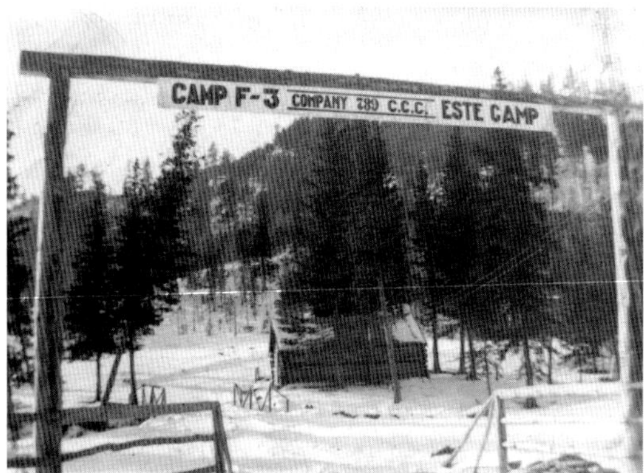

Left: CCC Camp Este. *Photo courtesy of Gabe Raba, from* The Civilian Conservation Corps: In and Around the Black Hills, *by Peggy Sanders.*

Below: CCC Camp Este. *Photo courtesy of Gabe Raba, from* The Civilian Conservation Corps: In and Around the Black Hills, *by Peggy Sanders.*

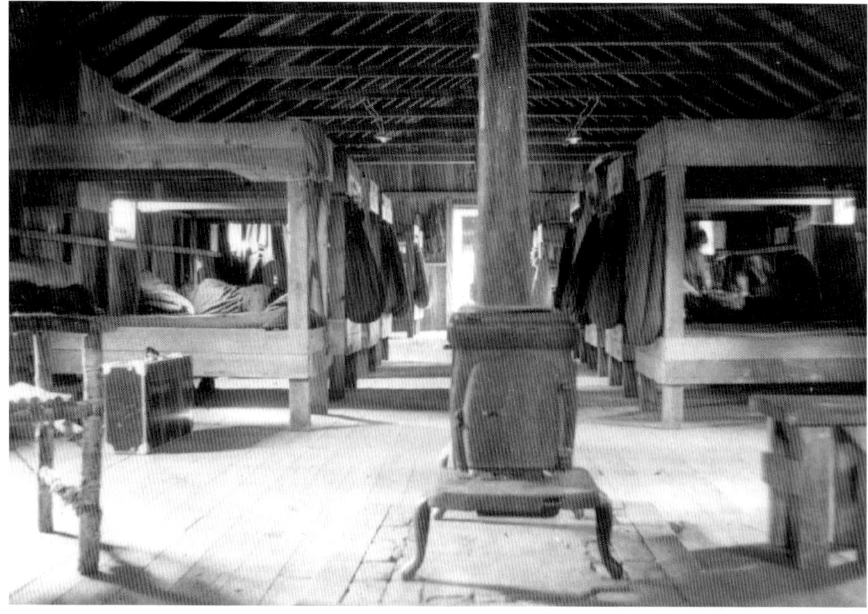

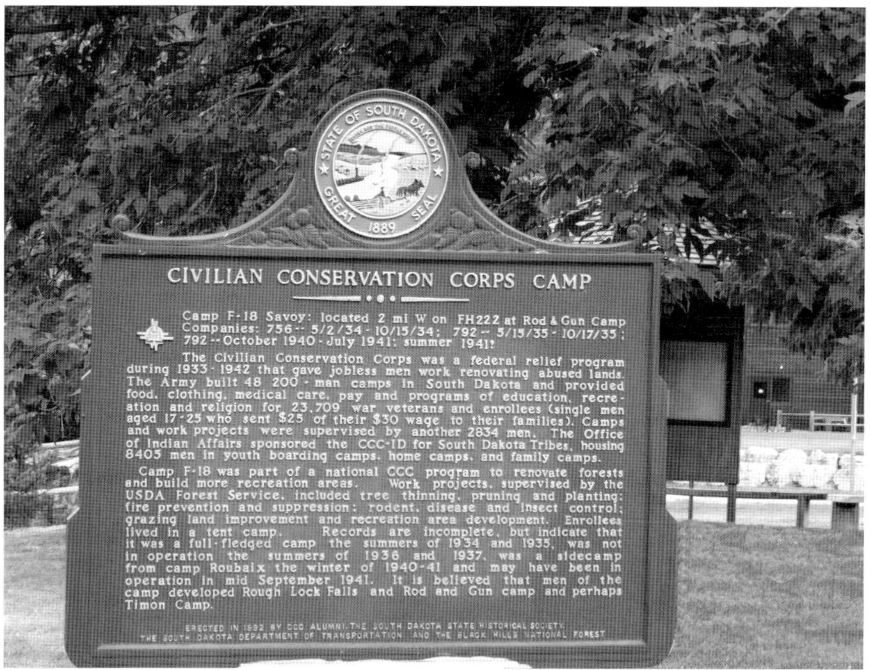

CCC historical marker. *Brad Tennant.*

1952

Groundbreaking for the Gavins Point Dam on the Missouri River takes place. The Pick-Sloan Plan, in conjunction with the Flood Control Act of 1944, authorized the dam's construction, which created Lewis and Clark Lake. The hydroelectric dam began operation in September 1956.

May 19, 1953

KELO-TV goes on the air, becoming South Dakota's first television station. Originally, all network and local broadcasts used film, which was aired from a transmitter located seven miles from the station. Not until November 1954 did KELO-TV begin using live broadcasts.

May 20, 1908

The "Official Proceedings" of the Western Federation of Miners shows a number of donations made for the approximately three thousand miners locked out by William Randolph Hearst and his Homestake Mining Company. The Copper Mining Union No. 203 and the Eureka Mining Union No. 151 joined other unions making donations for the miners.

May 21, 1980

Federal and state law enforcement officials raid Pam's Purple Door, a well-known brothel in Deadwood. Pam's Purple Door became the last openly known brothel to operate in Deadwood. Brothels had been a part of Deadwood dating to its earliest gold rush days of 1876.

May 22, 1936

Rapid City residents and guests dedicate Dinosaur Park on the city's Skyline Drive. The park features seven concrete dinosaurs that were constructed as part of a Works Progress Administration project.

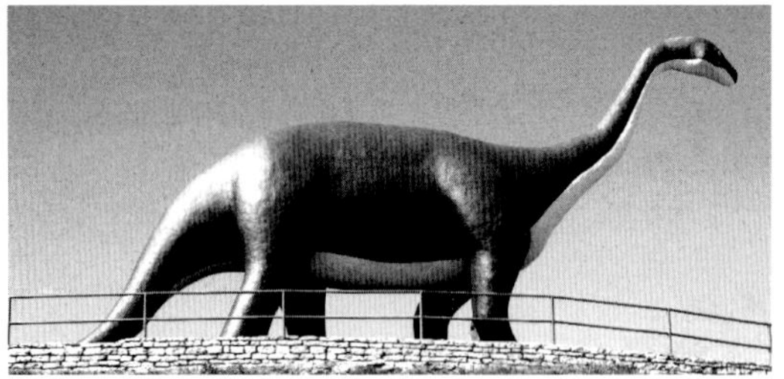

WPA Dinosaur Park. *Brigid Tennant.*

May 23, 1912

Speaking at a district development meeting, Joseph W. Parmley of Ipswich proposes a developed highway extending to Mobridge to replace the existing rough trail. Although Parmley's original plan called for a maintained

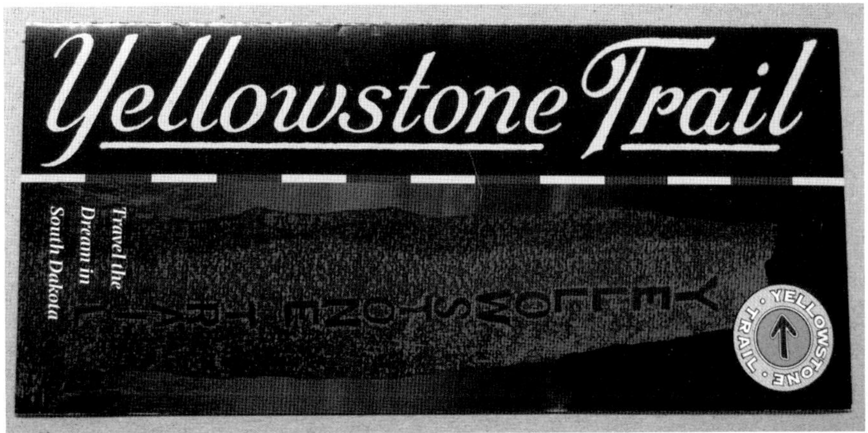

Yellowstone Trail brochure. *Brad Tennant.*

road from Aberdeen to Mobridge, he later envisioned a highway extending to Yellowstone National Park. Eventually, Parmley promoted a transcontinental highway from Massachusetts to Washington. Parmley's planned highway became known as the Yellowstone Trail.

May 24, 1991

The U.S. Congress approves the Niobrara Scenic River Designation Act of 1991, which added thirty-nine miles of the Missouri River, from Fort Randall Dam to Running Water, to "the wild and scenic rivers system."

May 25, 1942

As U.S. involvement in World War II begins to escalate, operation of an Army Air Corps Glider Pilot School in Aberdeen commences. Light airplanes, however, were used in lieu of actual gliders. The mission of the school was to train glider pilot students for combat operations.

May 26, 1906

The *Vernal (UT) Express* newspaper reports that a large band of Utes, estimated somewhere between three hundred to seven hundred individuals, left their assigned reservations and are heading to South Dakota. The Utes, which had been suffering deprivations, apparently intended to settle among the Sioux. When they eventually arrived at the area near Fort Meade, it became obvious that the Sioux were experiencing their own hardships. Eventually, most of the Utes returned to Utah; however, some did indeed remain with the Sioux.

May 27, 1910

The U.S. Congress passes an act to authorize the sale of surplus and non-allotted lands on the Pine Ridge Indian Reservation.

May 28, 1972

After more than five years of improvements, the National Park Service opens the Scenic Cave Tour route and visitor center at Jewel Cave. Although Jewel Cave had long been a destination for visitors, it was not until 1939 that the National Park Service placed a ranger at the national monument to conduct tours.

May 29, 1922

South Dakota Public Broadcasting begins radio programming for the first time. The University of South Dakota held the license, with the original call letters WEAJ, beginning in 1923. The call letters were later changed to KUSD in 1925.

May 30

1923

The "Cathedral of the Prairie" congregation in Hoven holds a special dedication mass, during which the name of the church changes from St. Bernard to St. Anthony of Padua Catholic Church. The Most Reverend Bishop Bernard Mahoney and thirty-one priests blessed the church, which Bishop Mahoney admired as a "magnificent temple of God that had been erected on these prairies." As part of the day's celebration, Reverend Father A.C. Helmbrecht is recognized for the twenty-fifth anniversary of his ordination. Construction of the church finished in 1921, and its congregation celebrated its first Christmas Mass in the church on December 25, 1921.

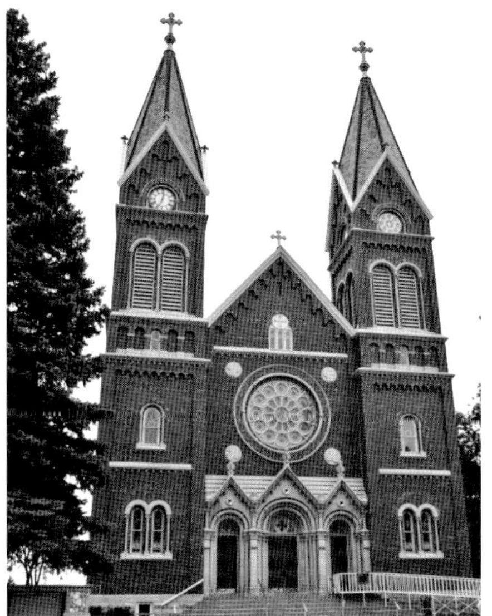

Left: St. Anthony of Padua Catholic Church, "Cathedral of the Prairie." *Brigid Tennant*.

Below: Hoven's "Cathedral of the Prairie." *Brigid Tennant*.

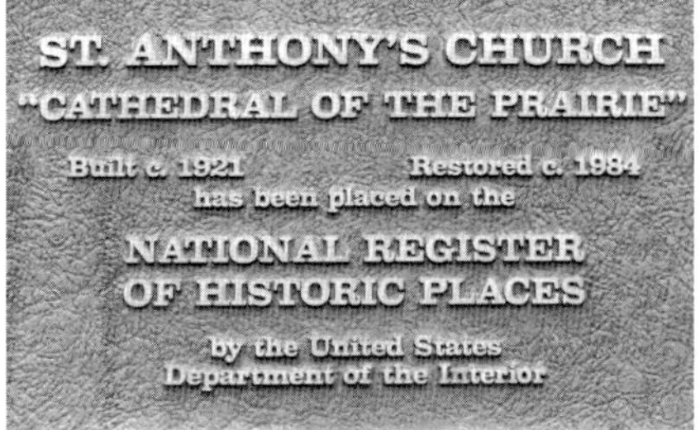

1998

An F4 tornado strikes the town of Spencer, killing six of the town's residents. Afterward, the National Weather Service reported that winds reached in excess of two hundred miles an hour, severely damaging structures throughout the community.

May 31, 2014

Matt Guthmiller of Aberdeen leaves Gillespie Field in El Cajon, California, as he begins his quest to become the youngest pilot to fly around the globe. Guthmiller successfully completed his flight in forty-four days, setting a world record as the youngest pilot to do so at the age of nineteen years, seven months and fifteen days.

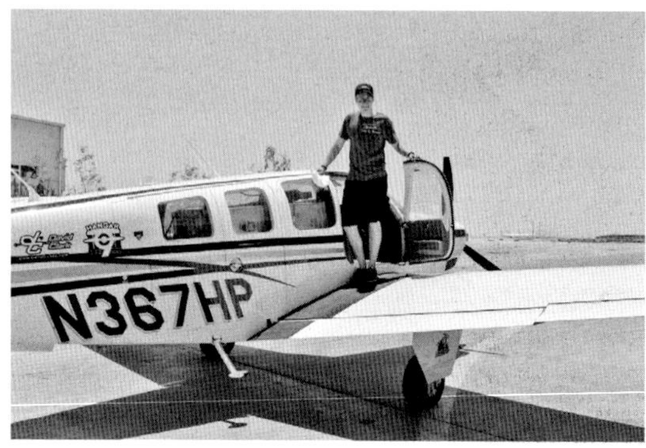

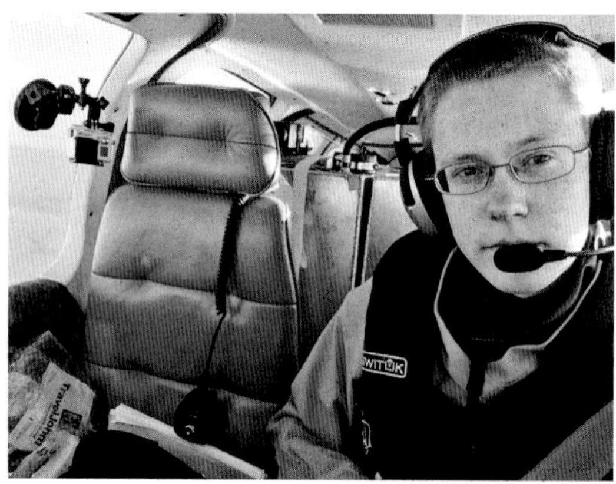

This page: Matthew Guthmiller. *Courtesy of Matthew Guthmiller.*

June

June is the "Moon of Making Fat," and the growing season is well under way. June events include the launching and decommissioning of the state's most famous namesake battleship, the start of another mountain monument, a grasshopper plague and the discovery of mammoth bones.

June 1, 1962

The U.S. Navy strikes the USS *South Dakota* from its Naval Vessel Register. The navy decommissioned the battleship in January 1947, after which it was placed at the Philadelphia Naval Shipyard. A little over four months later, it was sold for scrap.

June 2, 2004

Secretary of State Chris Nelson writes a letter to the clerk of the U.S. House of Representatives acknowledging that Stephanie Herseth unofficially won the special election to fill the at-large Congressional district. The seat became vacant after Representative William Janklow resigned after being convicted of vehicular manslaughter. The election results were soon made official, and Herseth took the oath of office the next day. The state's Congressional delegation of Senator Tom Daschle, Senator Tim Johnson and Congresswoman Stephanie Herseth marked the first time since 1937 that South Dakota had an all-Democratic delegation in Washington, D.C.

June 3

1949

The first blast takes place at Thunderhead Mountain, beginning Korczak Ziolkowski's monument to the Lakota leader Crazy Horse. A small group of individuals who were at the Battle of the Little Bighorn, where Lieutenant Colonel George A. Custer suffered defeat, attended the first blast ceremony. Chief Henry Standing Bear is credited with inviting Ziolkowski to construct a memorial to Crazy Horse.

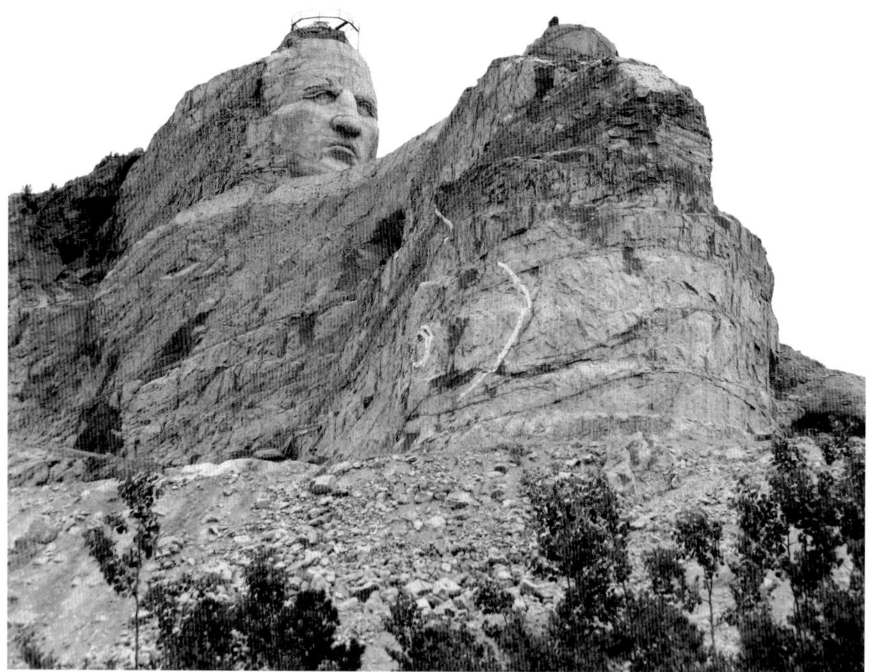

Crazy Horse. *Brad Tennant.*

1969

President Richard M. Nixon dedicates the Karl E. Mundt Library at General Beadle State College in Madison. Karl E. Mundt served five terms in the U.S. House of Representatives and four terms in the U.S. Senate. Today, General Beadle State College is Dakota State University, and the Karl E. Mundt Archives serves as the repository for Mundt's papers from his political career.

June 4, 1950

Saint Ann's Hospital in Watertown is dedicated. The order of Bernardine Sisters oversaw the hospital's management until 1973, when the Benedictine Sisters assumed the hospital's operations.

June 5, 1934

As automobiles become more common in American society, a Sioux Falls *Argus Leader* article reports that law enforcement officers are on the lookout for couples engaging in inappropriate behavior while parked in cars at Terrace and Sherman Parks.

June 6, 1890

Members of the Farmers' Alliance and the Knights of Labor hold a political convention in Huron with the intent of creating a new Independent Party. Convention attendees established party planks that included government ownership of railroads, a national income tax and the secret ballot. Since this convention preceded a similar Kansas convention the following week, many historians consider what became known as the Populist, or People's, Party to have originated with this South Dakota convention.

June 7, 1941

USS *South Dakota* (Battleship "X") is launched by the New York Shipbuilding Corporation in Camden, New Jersey. The *South Dakota* served in both the Pacific and Atlantic theaters and became the most decorated battleship of World War II. A memorial to the *South Dakota* and a gift shop are located in Sioux Falls.

June 8, 1902

Charles Ingalls dies of heart disease in De Smet. Charles was the father of Laura Ingalls Wilder of *Little House on the Prairie* fame. Not one to stay in a place too long, "Pa" Ingalls moved the family numerous times before finally settling in De Smet when it was still Dakota Territory.

June 9–10, 1972

Fifteen inches of rainfall leads to severe sudden flooding, causing the Canyon Lake Park Dam in Rapid City to fail. In the ensuing devastation, 238 residents were killed.

June 10, 2003

The Homestake Gold Mine closes entirely after having ceased production in January 2002. The mine dates to the 1876 Black Hills gold rush, when brothers Mose (or Moses) and Fred Manuel began looking for gold and staked their claim. California investors George Hearst, Lloyd Tevis and James Ben Ali Haggin later bought the mine for $70,000. At the time of its closing, it was the oldest, largest and deepest mine in the Western Hemisphere, having been in operation for more than 125 years.

June 11, 2011

A vehicle hits and kills a mountain lion in Connecticut. When the Forest Service Wildlife Genetics Laboratory in Missoula, Montana, conducted DNA tests, the results showed that the mountain lion's DNA matched that of the mountain lion population found in the Black Hills of western South Dakota. Additional DNA testing confirmed that samples collected in Minnesota and Wisconsin belonged to the same mountain lion. Authorities concluded that the animal had traveled more than 1,500 miles from South Dakota to Connecticut.

June 12, 1897

The *Chicago Tribune* publishes an article titled "Grasshoppers in South Dakota." According to the article, grasshoppers, or Rocky Mountain locusts, caused a great deal of damage in some counties. Aberdeen reported "ravages of grasshoppers," and farmers in eastern Spink County expressed concern over "the prevalence of grasshoppers in large numbers." Although only some counties reported the problem, there was a growing concern that the grasshoppers would take flight and spread to other locations.

June 13

1943

The deadliest air disaster in state history occurs when two B-17 bombers on a training flight collide over Miner County. The collision left eleven servicemen dead.

1953

Having arrived in the Black Hills on June 11, Dwight Eisenhower ends his vacation by dedicating Ellsworth Air Force Base near Rapid City. Eisenhower became the first president to arrive in the state by air. While in the Black

Hills, he stayed at the State Game Lodge at Custer State Park. He relaxed by fishing, and he spoke to the South Dakota Young Republican League.

1972

George McGovern, a U.S. senator from Mitchell, accepts the Democratic Party's nomination for president of the United States. Republican candidate Richard Nixon eventually defeated McGovern with 520 electoral votes to McGovern's 17.

1979

A U.S. Court of Claims decides in a 5–2 ruling that the 1877 act that seized the Black Hills from the Sioux was a violation of the Fifth Amendment. The U.S. Supreme Court later confirmed in *United States v. Sioux Nation of Indians* (1980) that the United States' taking of the Black Hills from the Sioux Indian Nation violated the 1868 Fort Laramie Treaty and the Fifth Amendment.

June 14–15, 1967

Almost four inches of rain in the upstream region of the Bad River creates severe flooding in Fort Pierre on June 18. The runoff increased the discharge of the Bad River, causing four to five feet of water to flood homes and businesses.

June 15

1924

Eight members of one family living near the Bijou Hills, and two other individuals near White Lake, are killed by a "South Dakota windstorm." Newspapers reported considerable wind damage to property and a variety of injuries.

1927

President Calvin Coolidge arrives in Rapid City by train. The president and his wife, Grace, stayed in South Dakota until their departure almost three months later on September 10. Coolidge initially planned on a short vacation in the Black Hills while the White House underwent renovation, but he became so enamored of the setting that he made the Black Hills his summer home.

June 16, 2003

According to information from the Private Corrections Working Group, Corplan Corrections of North Carolina announces that it is discontinuing a feasibility study to build a five-hundred-bed corrections facility at Huron.

June 17

1927

The first USS *South Dakota*, later renamed the USS *Huron*, is decommissioned.

1944

A tornado leaves eight dead in Wilmot. It is the deadliest tornado in state history.

June 18, 1916

President Woodrow Wilson orders the Fourth South Dakota Infantry Regiment mobilized in preparation for service along the Mexican border. Wilson decided to mobilize the Fourth Infantry Regiment after a March 9, 1916 attack by a group of Mexican irregulars that left nineteen Americans dead in Columbus, New Mexico. The regiment, consisting of soldiers from throughout the state, was ordered to San Benito, Texas, where the unit spent seven months along the Rio Grande River. On March 3, 1917, it was mustered out of federal service, only to be recalled a month later when the United States entered World War I.

June 19, 1883

Although statehood would not be gained for another six years, supporters of making the southern part of Dakota Territory a separate state meet in Huron. Wilmot Whitfield, chair of the convention's executive committee, opened the convention by reading the "Call for a gathering to create a constitution."

June 20, 1935

Four men convicted of robbing the First National Bank in Freeman are sentenced to life in prison. When authorities arrested the men in Rapid City, they were in the process of planning more robberies.

June 21

1954

The U.S. Congress approves an act authorizing payment of $8,124.29 to the South Dakota State Hospital for the Insane in Yankton "for compensation for services furnished Indian patients from the Rosebud and Pine Ridge Indian Agencies."

1977

Elvis Presley performs in Rapid City's new Rushmore Plaza Civic Center in connection with its grand opening. Presley's Rapid City performance came two months before his death.

June 22, 2009

Governor M. Michael Rounds and T. Denny Sanford dedicate the Sanford Underground Science and Engineering Laboratory at the Homestake Mine at Lead. The dedication ceremony for the laboratory took place in the former gold mine at a depth of more than 4,800 feet.

June 23, 1987

The U.S. Supreme Court, in a 7–2 decision, rules against the State of South Dakota in the case of *South Dakota v. Dole*. The case involved a 1984 federal law that authorized the withholding of 5 percent of federal highway funds if states did not raise their minimum legal drinking age to twenty-one. At the time, South Dakota's legal drinking age was nineteen.

June 24

1974

A bulldozer operator uncovers a mammoth tusk at a housing development in Hot Springs. Today, the Mammoth Site includes an enclosed facility where over five dozen mammoth remains dating back twenty-six thousand years ago have been uncovered. Although other prehistoric animal remains have also been found, the site is home to the world's largest Columbian mammoth exhibit and research center.

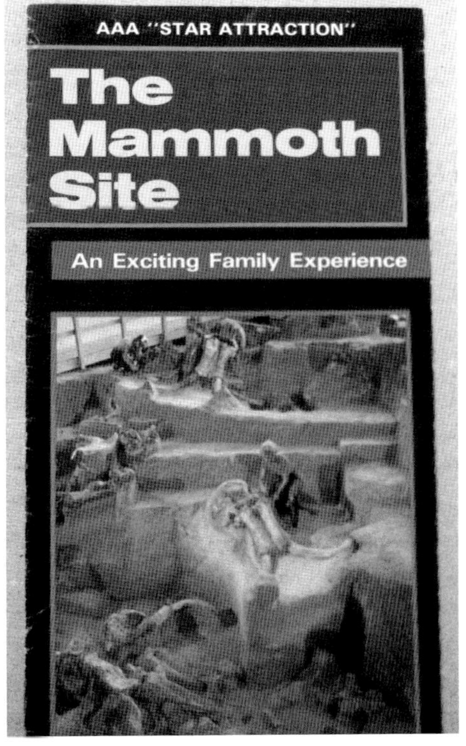

Mammoth Site brochure. *Brad Tennant.*

2003

This date became known as Tornado Tuesday—sixty-seven tornadoes were recorded in South Dakota within an eight-hour period. Fortunately, no fatalities occurred. However, a tornado destroyed the town of Manchester, South Dakota.

June 25, 1908

Governor Coe Crawford addresses a crowd as the cornerstone for the state capitol building is dedicated. The dedication ceremony included an opening prayer by Reverend John Askin, a Masonic rite led by Grand Master J.J. Davenport and addresses by Governor Crawford and William H.H. Beadle.

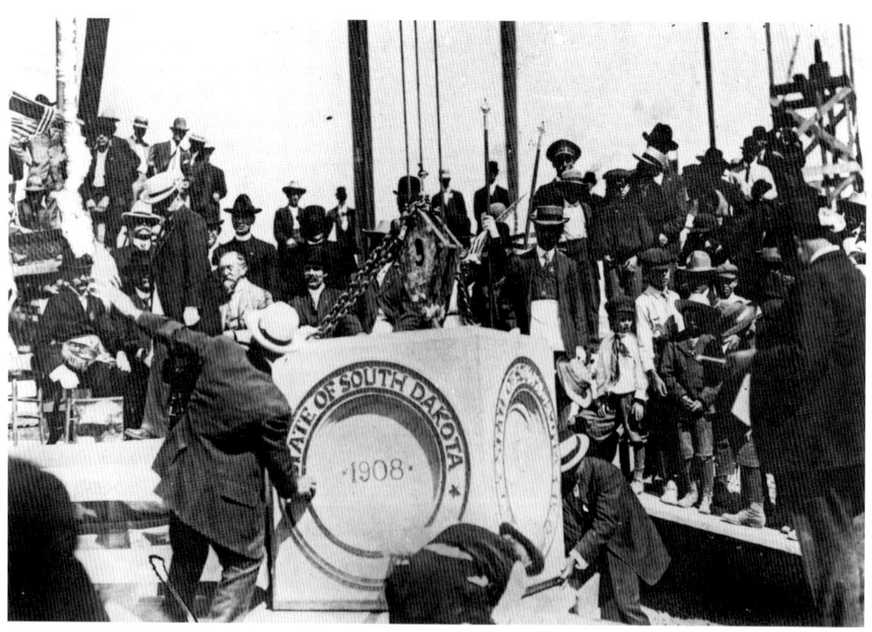

Capitol cornerstone dedication. *South Dakota State Historical Society.*

June 26, 1975

Two FBI agents, Jack Coler and Ronald Williams, are killed in the line of duty after being shot execution-style. Leonard Peltier, who was associated with the American Indian Movement, was tried in U.S. District Court in Fargo, North Dakota. He was convicted by a jury for the murders and sentenced to two consecutive life sentences.

June 27, 2013

Mount Rushmore is the site of a naturalization ceremony sponsored by the Mount Rushmore Society and the National Park Service. At the ceremony, 158 individuals from fifty-eight countries took the oath to become U.S. citizens.

June 28, 1894

Congress approves a bill introduced by U.S. senator James Kyle designating the first Monday of each September as a national holiday, to be called Labor Day. Kyle first served as a Populist but later switched to the Republican Party.

June 29

1911

President William Howard Taft issues a proclamation further opening the Pine Ridge and Rosebud Reservations for non-Indian settlement.

2006

Cecilia Fire Thunder, the first woman elected to lead the Oglala Sioux Tribe, is impeached. Controversy surrounded Fire Thunder's leadership when she openly opposed the state's restrictions on abortions by proposing a health clinic for women of the Pine Ridge Reservation who might seek such medical procedures.

June 30, 1942

The U.S. Congress votes to end the Civilian Conservation Corps program. During its existence, an estimated twenty-seven thousand men participated in conservation projects in camps throughout the state. As one of several major New Deal work programs, the young men who worked for CCC camps received a pay of thirty dollars a month, with twenty-five dollars being sent home to their families. The men kept the remaining five dollars for their use.

July

July is the "Moon of Red Cherries." It is a month that involved the hanging of a convicted murderer, a significant event for "The Star-Spangled Banner" and a whole community listed as a National Historic landmark. It is also the month when the state's highest temperature was recorded.

July 1, 1901

U.S. senator James Kyle passes away. The minister-turned-politician's health had been poor for the preceding several years of his life. The South Dakota state legislature originally elected Kyle as a Populist. Although Kyle retained his Populist affiliation throughout most of his career as a senator, he later switched to the Republican Party. Senator Kyle is credited with sponsoring legislation making Labor Day a national holiday.

July 2, 1939

Theodore Roosevelt's image on Mount Rushmore is dedicated.

July 3

1909

Emil Victor commits a horrendous mass murder and robbery near Rudolph in Brown County. A jury found the nineteen-year-old guilty of killing James Christie, his wife and daughter and a boy who worked for the Christie family. The jury sentenced Victor to death by hanging. Having secured a building permit from the City of Aberdeen, Brown County arranged for a scaffold to be built in the jail yard. Victor was hanged for his vicious crimes on November 16, 1909.

1991

President George H.W. Bush attends a dedication ceremony recognizing the fiftieth anniversary of the completion of Mount Rushmore.

July 4

1892

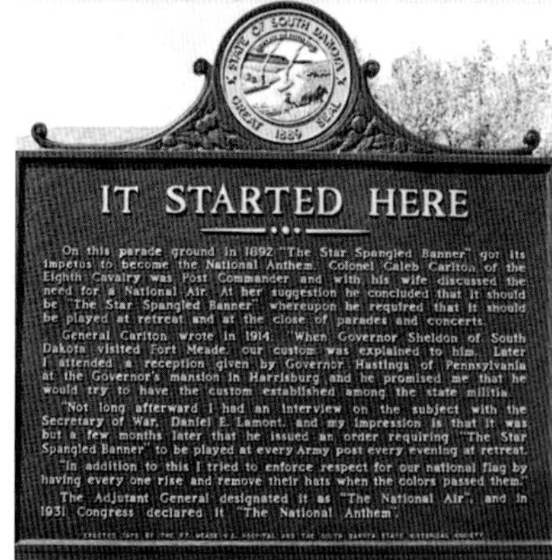

Fort Meade, "It Started Here." *By Brad L. Jones, Creative Commons. https://commons.wikimedia.org/w/index.php?curid=37175583.*

At the conclusion of an Independence Day concert by the Fort Meade regimental band, Colonel Caleb H. Carlton, the commanding officer at the fort, orders that "The Star-Spangled Banner" be played. Carlton and his wife, Sadie, had discussed the need for an appropriate song to be performed on significant official occasions. Sadie is credited with specifically suggesting "The Star-Spangled Banner." Although many events throughout the United States featured the song, Colonel Carlton is acknowledged for having it played each night at retreat—a practice that then spread to other military posts. In 1931, Congress officially made "The Star-Spangled Banner" the national anthem.

1919

Mount Roosevelt Friendship Tower is dedicated. Deadwood sheriff Seth Bullock built the tower as a legacy of his friendship with Theodore Roosevelt. In 2005, the National Park Service placed the Friendship

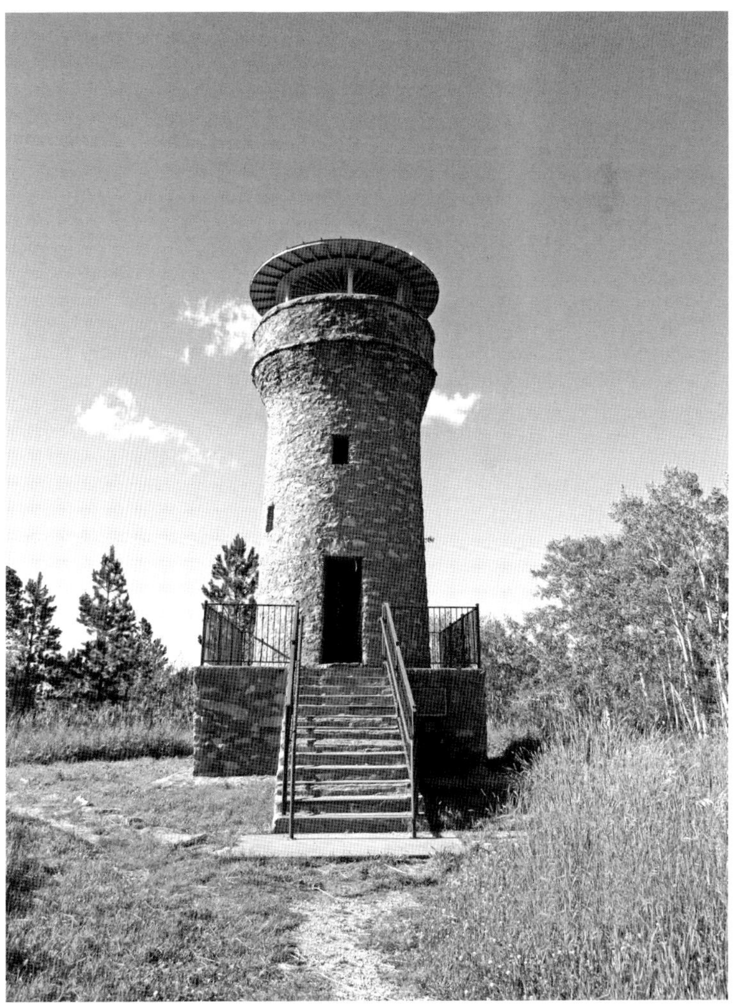

Mount Roosevelt Friendship Tower. *Brigid Tennant.*

Tower in the National Register of Historic Places. This monument became the first in the country to honor Theodore Roosevelt. The tower is thirty-one feet tall and is located on top of Mount Roosevelt (elevation 5,680 feet), giving visitors a remarkable view overlooking the Black Hills National Forest.

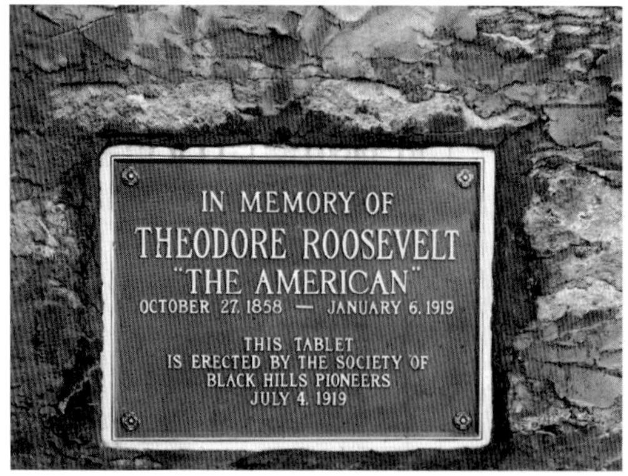

Mount Roosevelt Friendship Tower memorial plaque. *Brigid Tennant.*

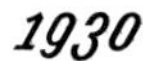

1930

Dedication of Washington's image on Mount Rushmore.

1961

Founded in 1876 as part of the Black Hills gold rush, Deadwood is designated as a National Historic Landmark. Deadwood was home to well-known historical figures such as Wild Bill Hickok and Calamity Jane. A historic mining town, Deadwood became the only city in South Dakota to allow legalized gambling (limited card games and slot machines) after voters approved a 1988 initiated constitutional amendment. In 2014, voters approved adding keno and craps to the city's gaming options. According to the South Dakota Constitution, gambling revenue is to be applied

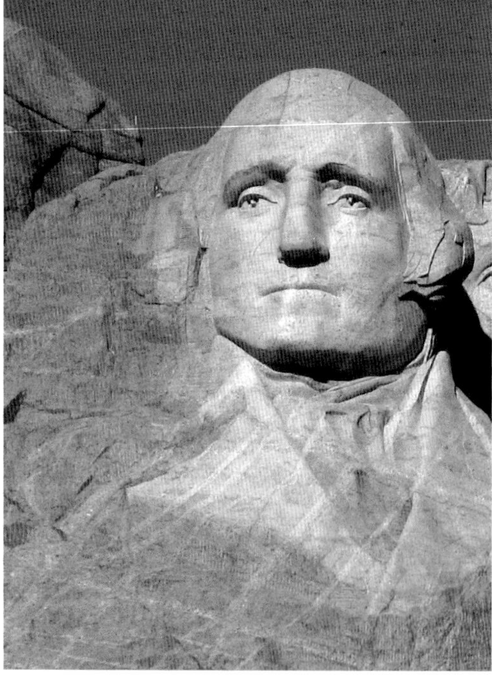

George Washington, Mount Rushmore. *Brad Tennant.*

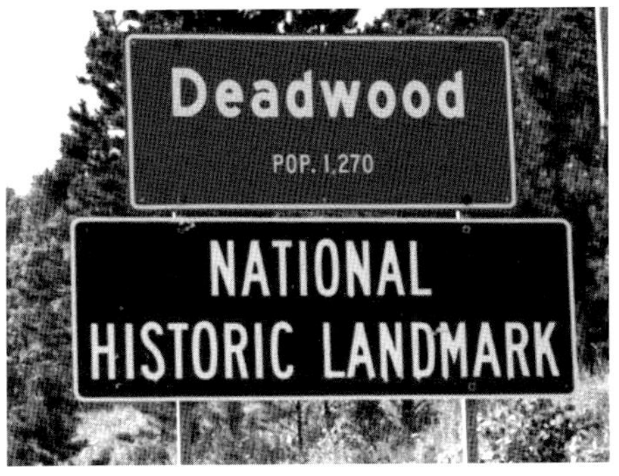

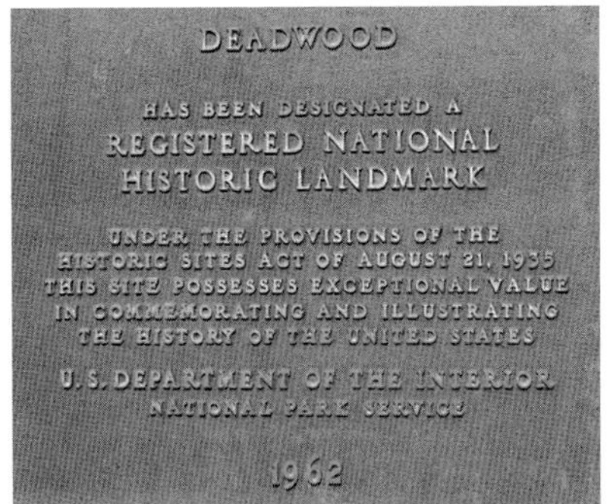

Left: Deadwood Historic Landmark. *Brigid Tennant*; *right*: Deadwood Historic Landmark plaque. *Brigid Tennant.*

toward historic preservation in order to maintain the town's National Historic Landmark status.

July 5, 1936

The temperature at Gann Valley, Buffalo County, reaches a South Dakota record high of 120 degrees. The state record was tied at Usta in 2006.

July 6–7, 1999

President Bill Clinton arrives at Ellsworth Air Force Base for a planned visit to the Pine Ridge Indian Reservation. Clinton briefly visited Mount Rushmore and the Crazy Horse Memorial before going to Pine Ridge on July 7. Clinton's visit was part of a national tour of economically underdeveloped areas to discuss housing and jobs programs.

July 6, 1942

The first group of servicemen to be stationed at the Army Radio Technical Training School in Sioux Falls begins to arrive. Starting in March 1942, almost six thousand men worked to construct the infrastructure of the base in order to have it completed as quickly as possible. At the peak of its training operations, over twenty-seven thousand men were stationed at the base and took classes offered on a rotational basis throughout the day and night. The training focused mainly on proficiency in Morse code and radio communications. Training ceased when the Radio Technical Training School closed in May 1945. Deactivation of the base occurred later that year.

July 7, 2016

A Delta Air Lines jet mistakenly lands at Ellsworth Air Force Base instead of its intended destination ten miles away at the Rapid City Regional Airport.

July 8, 1999

The Dakota Mining Corporation declares bankruptcy. Since the Dakota Mining Company was the parent company of the Brohm Mining Corporation, Brohm abandoned environmental cleanup plans for a mine that it had been operating. Brohm had a $6 million reclamation bond; however, due to the bankruptcy, the state had to take action to prevent polluted water from running into nearby streams. The Minneapolis *Star Tribune* reported that the situation "cost taxpayers more than $105 million" and that the amount continues to grow.

July 9, 1936

According to the National Weather Service, this date marks the beginning of nine consecutive days (July 9–17) that Sioux Falls reached temperatures of one hundred degrees or higher.

July 10, 2007

The National Science Foundation selects the former Homestake Gold Mine in Lead as the site for the Deep Underground Science and Engineering Laboratory. Governor Mike Rounds signed the papers in April 2006 transferring the title to the State of South Dakota from Barrick Gold, Inc., which owned the mine. The site now operates as the Sanford Underground Research Facility.

July 11

1912

Construction begins on what became known as the Yellowstone Trail highway. J.W. Parmley presented his proposal at a May regional development meeting in Ipswich, citing the increasing use of automobiles and the need for properly developed roads. His original plan involved a maintained stretch of road through three counties. By October, however, organizers decided to develop the road as far as Yellowstone National Park. Eventually, the Yellowstone Trail became U.S. Highway 12, extending from Plymouth, Massachusetts, to Seattle, Washington.

2007

Elijah Page becomes the second convicted murderer to be executed by the State of South Dakota and the first person to be executed in the state by lethal injection. Sixty years earlier, in 1947, George Sitts became the only person to be executed in South Dakota by the electric chair.

July 12, 1972

At the Democratic Party's national convention, U.S. senator George McGovern is nominated to be its presidential candidate. McGovern had become an outspoken critic of U.S. involvement in Vietnam. In the November election, incumbent Richard Nixon soundly defeated McGovern by an electoral vote of 520 to 17. McGovern won only the state of Massachusetts and the District of Columbia.

July 13, 1893

Governor Charles Sheldon participates in events at the World's Columbian Exposition in Chicago in recognition of "South Dakota Day." The day included the dedication of the South Dakota building, which housed a variety of exhibits highlighting the state. Due to the state's treasury troubles, private citizens provided much of the financing for the building.

July 14, 2014

Matthew Guthmiller becomes the youngest person to fly solo around the world. According to the *Guinness Book of World Records*, Guthmiller, who flew a 1981 Beech A36 Bonanza from May 31 to July 14, 2014, completed his circumnavigation at the age of nineteen years, seven months and fifteen days.

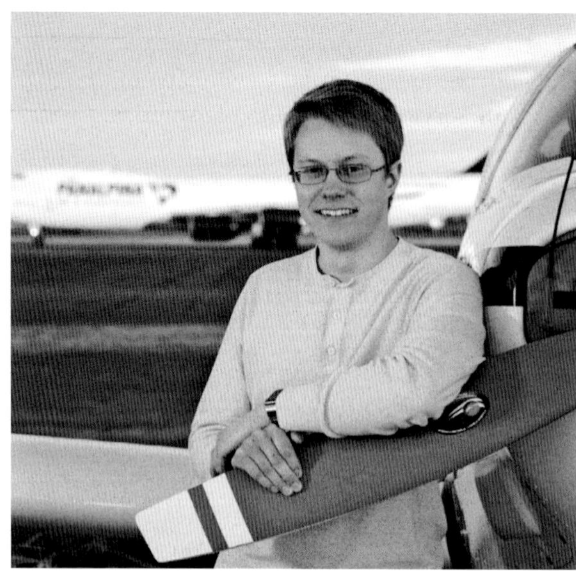

Matthew Guthmiller. *Courtesy of Matthew Guthmiller.*

July 15, 2006

South Dakota ties its highest recorded temperature of 120 degrees Fahrenheit at Usta in the northwestern region of the state. Previously, the highest recorded temperature was at Gann Valley in 1936.

July 16, 1918

The Fall River overflows, flooding parts of Hot Springs and resulting in serious road and property damage.

July 17

1925

The South Dakota American Legion holds its annual convention in Milbank. It was at this convention that members passed a resolution proposing American Legion Baseball. The national American Legion organization later passed the state's resolution. A monument in Milbank proudly acknowledges the role of the town as the birthplace of American Legion Baseball: "In this city on July 17, 1925, by action of the South Dakota Department of the American Legion, the nationwide organization of Legion Junior Baseball was first proposed as a program of service to the youth of America."

1991

The National Park Service officially recognizes the Verendrye and Fort Pierre Chouteau sites as National Historic Landmarks. The Verendrye brothers, François and Louis-Joseph, left a lead plate on a hill overlooking the Missouri River near present-day Fort Pierre. The plate includes the following text: "In the twenty-sixth year of the reign of Louis XV, the most illustrious Lord, the Lord Marquis of Beauharnios, 1741, Pierre Gaultier De La Verendrye placed this." With this action, he claimed the region as a French territory. The back of the lead plate states that it was "Placed by the Chevalier Verendrye,

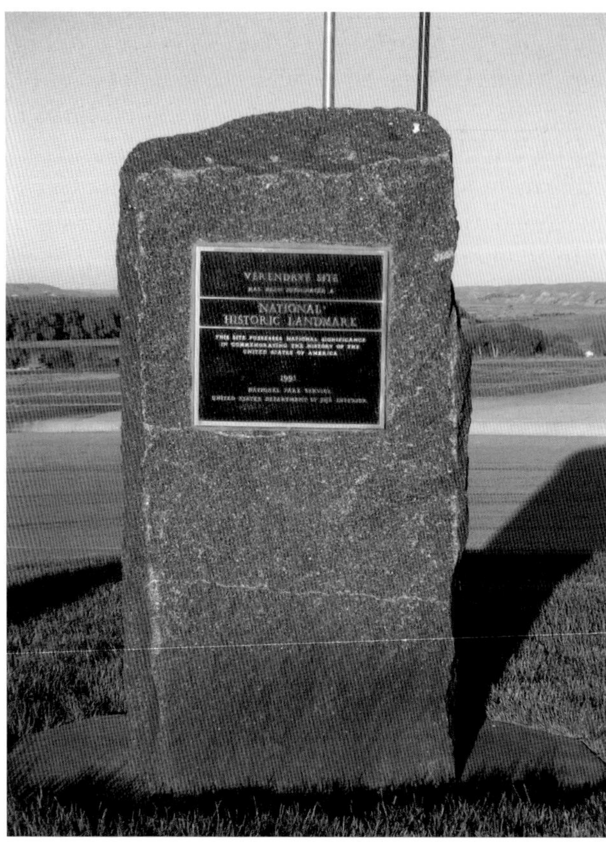

Left: Verendrye National Historic Landmark. *Brigid Tennant.*

Below: Verendrye Monument. *Brad Tennant.*

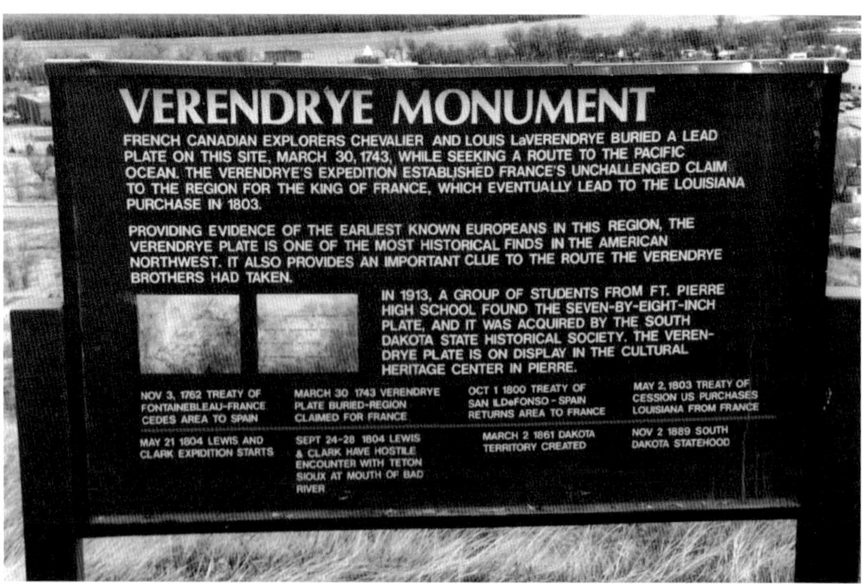

Louis La Londette, and A. Miotte. 30 March 1743." This is the oldest record of white men in what is now South Dakota. Schoolchildren found the six- by eight-inch plate by chance in 1913. It is now housed at the South Dakota State Historical Society's Cultural Heritage Center in Pierre.

Named for Pierre Chouteau Jr. and established in 1832, the Fort Pierre trading post became an integral part of the operations for John Jacob Astor's American Fur Company. In addition to numerous explorers and fur traders who visited the area, such famed artists as George Catlin, Karl Bodmer and John James Audubon captured images of post activities, the landscape, wildlife and the impact of the early fur trade on the native populations.

July 18, 1907

The Chicago, Milwaukee, St. Paul & Pacific Railroad completes its rail line connecting Chamberlain to Rapid City. The railroad company used a pontoon bridge to cross the Missouri River. Two days later, on July 20, 1907, the first train arrived in Rapid City from Chicago.

July 19, 1964

Recognized as one of the most significant archaeological sites for prehistoric cultures in South Dakota, the Crow Creek site becomes a designated National Historic Landmark. The village site, associated with the Coalescent culture, is known for the discovery of nearly five hundred individuals who were killed as the result of an attack on the site around AD 1325. The remains were found buried at the bottom of a trench that once served as a line of defense for the village.

July 20, 1952

Construction having begun in 1946, the Fort Randall Dam on the Missouri River experiences its closure and prepares for operation. The dam, which created Lake Francis Case, began producing electricity two years later.

July 21, 1904

South Dakota governor Charles Herreid attends the christening and launching of the first USS *South Dakota*. Herreid's daughter Grace christened the battleship and pressed the button launching the vessel into the water. It was commissioned in 1908 and decommissioned in 1927. Unlike the first two battleships named for the state, the third and most recent USS *South Dakota* will be a submarine. It is scheduled to join the U.S. Navy's fleet in 2018.

July 22, 1915

The Nebraska Telephone Company makes an application to the South Dakota Board of Railroad Commissioners requesting "authority to charge certain reduced rate for telephone service at schools and lodge rooms at their various exchanges in South Dakota." The board of railroad commissioners is now the South Dakota Public Utilities Commission.

July 23

1894

A statue of General John Logan is dedicated on the grounds of the South Dakota State Veteran's Home in Hot Springs. Logan served in the Union army during the Civil War, and he later played a major role in the creation of the Grand Army of the Republic (GAR). On March 3, 1868, Logan issued General Order No. 11, which called for a national day of remembrance for those who died during the Civil War. According to Logan, this day of remembrance was to be acknowledged annually on May 30. Originally known as Decoration Day, it is now known as Memorial Day.

1898

After six weeks of training, the First South Dakota Infantry departs San Francisco on two ships headed for the Philippines in connection with what

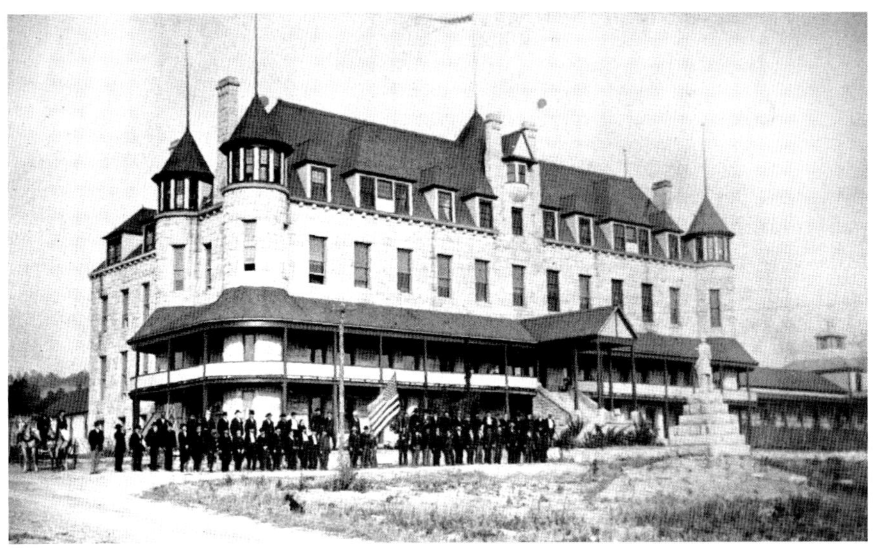

John A. Logan statue dedication. *Photo by W.R. Cross, courtesy of Pioneer Museum, from* Fall River County and Hot Springs: 125 Years, *by Peggy Sanders.*

became known as the Philippine-American War. The unit, which was formally called the First South Dakota Infantry, United States Volunteers, reached the Philippines a little over seven weeks later.

July 24, 1978

Governor Richard Kneip resigns in order to become the U.S. ambassador to Singapore, having been appointed by President Jimmy Carter. Kneip had served two two-year terms as governor. After voters approved amending the state constitution in 1972, he was elected to a four-year term in 1974. Consequently, Kneip became the first governor to be elected three times.

July 25, 1970

The Prayer Rock Museum in Britton opens. The museum is named for a 1,873-pound prayer rock used by early American Indians. The prayer rock has a variety of impressions carved into it, including handprints, common features of prayer rocks found across the northern plains. The Prayer Rock was moved from a nearby farm to the Prayer Rock Museum, where it remains today.

July 26, 1934

Internal Revenue Service agents conduct a raid in Yankton County, arresting ten men. Although the charges against the men were for liquor tax evasion, officials said that they were part of "a moonshine and alcohol syndicate" associated with what was at the time the largest syndicate operation in the state.

July 27, 2015

A storm drops hailstones ranging from one to three inches in size onto the community of Custer. By the time the storm finished, the ground had hail approximately six inches deep.

July 28, 1934

A three-man crew reaches an altitude of 60,613 feet in *Explorer I*, the world's largest balloon at the time. *Explorer I* cast off at 5:45 a.m. from a carefully selected site in the Black Hills that became known as the Stratobowl. Lorena Berry, the wife of Governor Tom Berry, had the honor of christening the balloon. The National Geographic Society co-sponsored the flight with the U.S. Army Corps. As it began its descent, *Explorer I* started to tear. Eventually, the crew, consisting of Major William E. Kepner, First Lieutenant Orvil A. Anderson and Captain Albert W. Stevens, parachuted to safety. This was the first of three notable flights originating from the Stratobowl to establish world records for manned balloons. The flights are considered to be essential to the start of the space age.

July 29–30, 1945

The USS *South Dakota*, along with other Third Fleet and British battleships, destroyers and cruisers, engages in two days of attacks on Hamamatsu, Honshu. The Japanese island of Honshu is about 125 miles from Tokyo, and Hamamatsu served as an important industrial city. *New York Times* correspondent George Jones later reported that one thousand tons of bombshells struck the city during the July 30 attack alone. For security reasons, the navy wanted to keep the identity of the Third Fleet's lead ship anonymous, so reports often referred to the USS *South Dakot*a simply as "Battleship X." Information provided by the USS *South Dakota* Memorial in Sioux Falls states that it is "a tribute to the 114 officers and 2,240 enlisted sailors" who represented all forty-eight states in their service on board the battleship named for the nation's fortieth state.

July 31, 1995

Dr. Jon Green becomes the fifteenth superintendent of the South Dakota School for the Deaf in Sioux Falls. According to historical information from the SDSD website, Green's nine-year tenure at the school was highlighted by several notable accomplishments, including the implementation of a bilingual education program and the establishment of a "Friends of the SDSD" Foundation.

August

A few of the occurrences during this month in South Dakota history are connected to events from territorial days. Specific events involve Calamity Jane and Jack McCall, who were both figures from the Wild West days of early Deadwood. In addition, Sturgis began hosting motorcyclists from around the world. August also features a Tyrannosaurus rex named Sue and the renaming of the state's highest peak. This is the "Moon When the Cherries Turn Black" and when the fruit ripens.

August 1, 1903

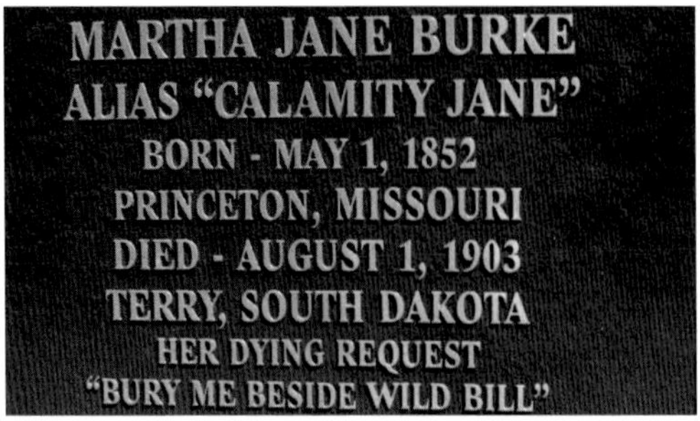

Calamity Jane Burial Site at Mount Moriah Cemetery. *Brigid Tennant.*

Calamity Jane dies. According to popular legend, Martha Jane Canary (Burke) wanted to be buried by Wild Bill Hickok in Deadwood's Mount Moriah Cemetery. There is, however, little to substantiate this claim or that Calamity Jane and Will Bill Hickok even knew each other very well on a personal basis.

August 2, 1876

In 1960, a historical marker placed in Yankton, titled "Trial of Jack McCall for Murder of Wild Bill," commemorates the events connected with Wild Bill Hickok's death. According to the historical maker:

> *At Deadwood on August 2, 1876, Jack McCall shot "Wild Bill" Hickok in the back of his head. When a vigilante court tried him, he claimed Bill had killed his brother and the vigilantes let him go. Later, due to his boasting, at Laramie City, US Marshall Balcombe of Nebraska arrested him and turned him over to US Marshal Burdick of Dakota. In October a grand jury indicted him and he was tried December 4-5-6, 1876, found guilty by a jury before Trial Judge Peter C. Shannon who sentenced him to hang.*

August 3–4, 1900

Bangor becomes the site for the sale of town lots in the new community of Selby. The Walworth County seat had been in Bangor for sixteen years, but the Milwaukee Railroad Company laid its tracks four miles north of town. As in other cases, the decision of the railroad company to bypass a community often meant its doom while benefiting other communities. As a result, Selby eventually replaced Bangor as the county seat.

August 5, 1916

The *Commercial West*, a publication covering news related to investment securities, banking and grain and milling, reports that for the first time since South Dakota's gaining statehood, "the state treasury at the end of the fiscal year 1916 had a surplus."

August 6, 1949

George T. Mickelson declares a coyote named Tootsie as "South Dakota's Official Animal." Fred Borsch, of Deadwood, acquired Tootsie as a pup in 1947 and taught the coyote to howl while Borsch sang. Together, Borsch and Tootsie made a record, participated in numerous public events and even visited the White House.

August 7, 1973

The Earth Resources Observation and Science Data Center is dedicated. The facility, which is located west of Garretson, has the largest mainframe computer in South Dakota. EROS is one of the largest computer facilities used by the U.S. Geological Survey, a bureau of the Department of the Interior. Today, approximately six hundred government and contracted employees work with the EROS Center. The facility officially began its operations in January 1974.

August 8, 1892

Father Robert Haire continues his endorsement of a state constitutional amendment allowing for the legislative methods of the initiative and referendum in an editorial column in the *Dakota Ruralist*. Haire promoted the initiative and referendum as a means of direct democracy because, as he stated in the column, "there would be no humbugging in committees as now, no secret sculduggery [*sic*], and passing bills at the last hour of the legislature." In 1898, South Dakota became the first state to adopt both measures, and Haire became known as the "Father of the Initiative and Referendum."

August 9, 1997

Attendees at the Sturgis Motorcycle Rally and pay-per-viewers are entertained by the theatrics of a professional wrestling event called Road

Wild. The event was first held in 1996 and had its final occurrence the following year.

August 10, 1927

President Calvin Coolidge makes the opening comments at the Mount Rushmore dedication ceremony:

> *We have come here to dedicate a cornerstone that was laid by the hand of the Almighty. On this towering wall of Rushmore, in the heart of the Black Hills, is to be inscribed a memorial which will represent some of the outstanding features of four of our Presidents, laid on by the hand of a great artist in sculpture. This memorial will crown the height of land between the Rocky Mountains and the Atlantic seaboard, where coming generations may view it for all time.*

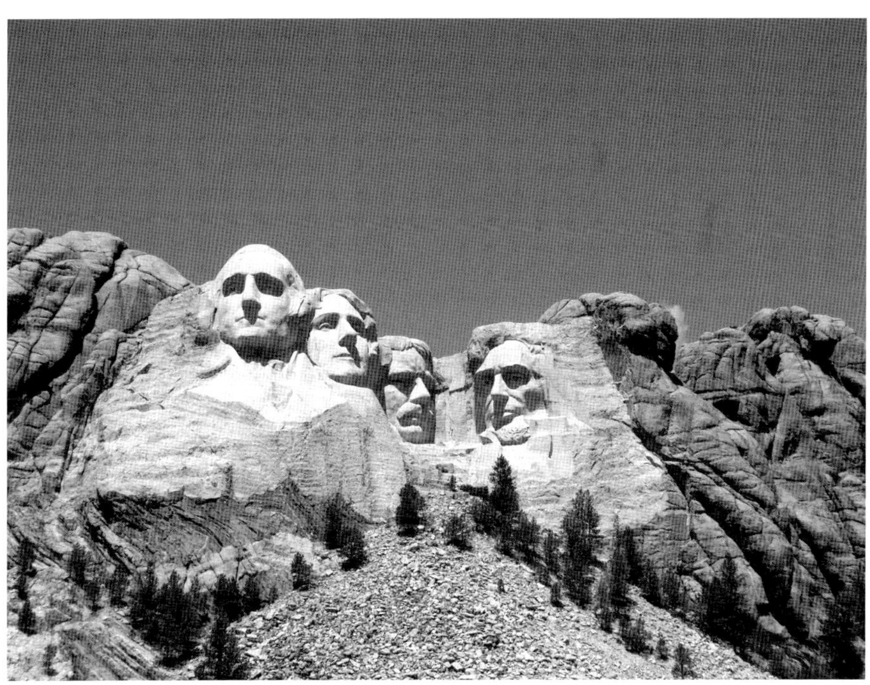

Mount Rushmore. *Brad Tennant.*

August 11

1952

The U.S. Post Office Department issues a three-cent Mount Rushmore Memorial stamp commemorating the twenty-fifth anniversary of the landmark's dedication.

2016

The Federal Board of Geographic Names votes to change the name of Harney Peak to Black Elk Peak. At 7,242 feet, the peak is regarded as the highest geographic elevation east of the Rocky Mountains. In 1857, Lieutenant G.K. Warren conducted a topographical survey of the Black Hills and named Harney Peak in honor of General William S. Harney. Since Harney fought in the Sioux conflicts of the 1850s, he is often held accountable for the deaths of Sioux men, women and children. As a result, the Board of Geographic Names changed the name to Black Elk Peak in recognition of the well-known Lakota spiritual leader whose life was the subject of John Neihardt's book *Black Elk Speaks*.

August 12

1907

President Theodore Roosevelt issues "Proclamation 771—Opening of Lower Brule Indian Reservation Lands" in accordance with the act of Congress authorizing the same, which passed on April 21, 1906.

1990

Sue Hendrickson, working with the Black Hills Institute of Geological Research, discovers the remains of a Tyrannosaurus rex near Faith in the Hell Creek Formation. The find, which later became known as "Sue," in honor of Hendrickson, represented the largest and most complete

"Faith—T-rex Capital of the World." *Brigid Tennant.*

Tyrannosaurus rex remains found at the time.

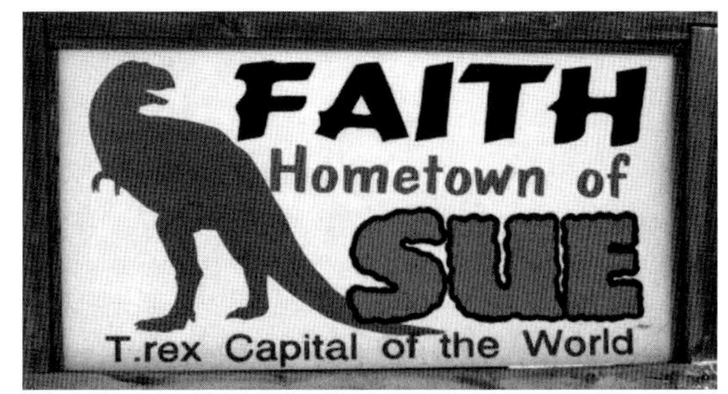

August 13, 2007

United States Bill S.975, allowing "for an interstate forest fire protection program for the Great Plains region" and sponsored by U.S. senator John Thune, is signed into law.

August 14, 1938

The first Black Hills Classic for motorcycles is held in Sturgis. The event featured a race with nine participants. The name of the Classic was later changed to the Sturgis Motorcycle Rally. The 2000 rally set an attendance record, with approximately 600,000 attendees.

August 15, 1911

A Hardangerlaget is founded at a meeting in Sioux Falls. The society is named for people who have connections to Hardanger, Norway. Given the number of immigrants to southeastern South Dakota in the early 1900s from the Hardanger region, organizers thought that such a society would be an appropriate way for people to share old country traditions and maintain friendships.

August 16, 2003

Longtime politician William Janklow fatally hits a motorcyclist with his car when he goes through an intersection in rural Moody County. Janklow, a U.S. representative at the time, previously served as the state's attorney general and governor. Janklow holds the record for being governor longer than anybody in state history, having served four four-year terms. His conviction of manslaughter in the traffic accident led to his resignation from Congress.

August 17, 1962

President John F. Kennedy dedicates the Oahe Dam, which, at the time, was the largest earth-rolled dam in the world. The Oahe Dam became the fifth of the six dams to be constructed on the Missouri River, four of which are in South Dakota. In his dedication speech, Kennedy stated:

> *Too often we take for granted these miracles of engineering and milestones in river development. Too often we see no connection between this dam and our nation's prosperity, our national security and our leadership of those nations who cherish their freedom. But the facts of the matter are that this dam, and many more like it, are as essential to the expansion and growth of the American economy as any measure the Congress is considering on taxes or unemployment—and this dam and the others like it are as essential to our national strength and security as any military alliance or missile complex.*

August 18, 1994

The U.S. Fish and Wildlife Service announces plans to reintroduce black-footed ferrets into the Badlands. Given that the southwestern region of the state has an abundance of prairie dog towns, the success of reintroducing black-footed ferrets is promising, as prairie dogs offer an abundant food source.

August 19

1909

President William Howard Taft authorizes the opening of the Cheyenne River and Standing Rock Indian Reservations to non-Indian settlement.

1943

The Red Cross/USO Canteen at the Chicago, Milwaukee & St. Paul Railroad depot in Aberdeen begins serving pheasant sandwiches to servicemen and women passing through on troop trains. Volunteers served more than 586,000 troops from August 1943 to March 1946.

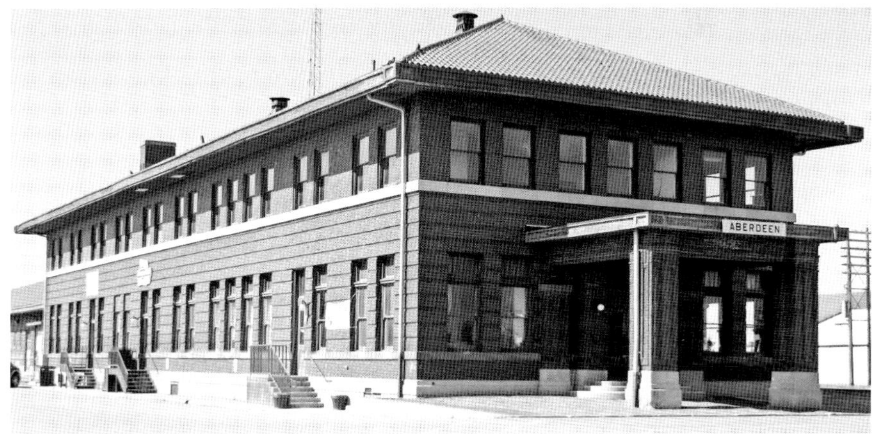

Chicago, Milwaukee & St. Paul Railroad depot. *Brad Tennant.*

August 20, 2002

Officials continue battling a three-week fire that is within four miles of Mount Rushmore. Although the national monument was not in immediate danger, several communities were evacuated, as the fire had already burned approximately ten thousand acres.

August 21, 1954

The new site of Medicine Rock is dedicated along U.S. Highway 212 in Gettysburg. The forty-ton prayer rock served as a common landmark near the Missouri River until the Oahe Dam created Lake Oahe; it became apparent that the rising water threatened to inundate Medicine Rock. Medicine Rock contains the man-made markings of human footprints, a hand and the tracks of a bear. In 1825, General Henry Atkinson and Major Benjamin O'Fallon made the first recorded visit to the boulder. On June 28, 1864, hostile warriors shot and killed Captain John Feilner, a naturalist under the command of General Alfred Sully, after he visited the boulder. Other famous visitors included Lieutenant Colonel George Custer and his wife, Elizabeth, in 1873. Medicine Rock remained at its site along Highway 212 until 1989, when it was moved to the Dakota Sunset Museum in Gettysburg.

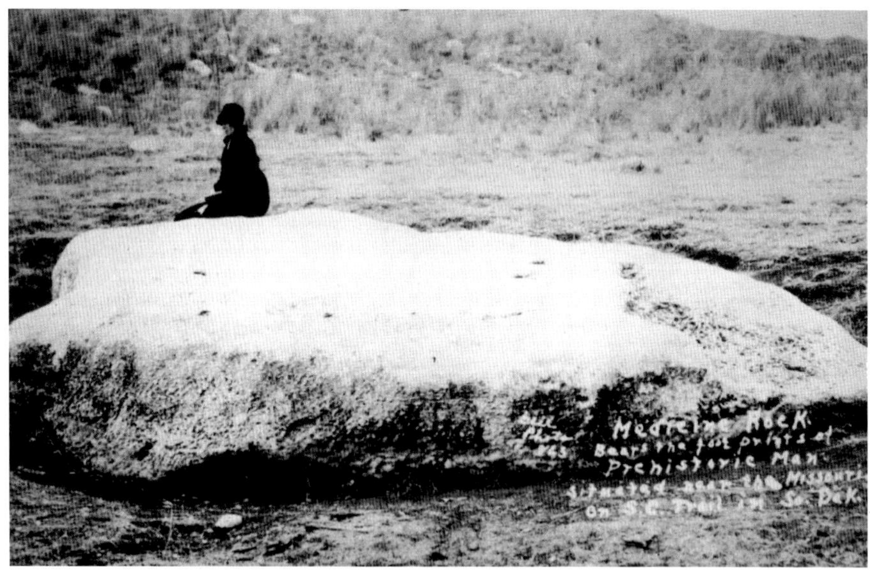

"Medicine Rock. Bears the foot prints of prehistoric man. Situated near the Missouri on S.C. Trail in So. Dak." Photographer unknown. *Brad Tennant personal collection.*

August 22, 1953

Ramona hosts its fifth annual horse show. According to Ramona centennial history, the event is traced to Father Paul Quinn, an avid horse lover and one of the founders of the Spur and Lariat Club. The centennial history reported that "the fifth annual horse show…featured the following events: Matched Pairs, Cigar Race, Pop Race, Flag Race, Bending Race (poles), Musical Chair, Tire Race, Relay Race, Dizzy Race, Balloon Race, Potato Race, Sack Race, Clover Leaf (barrels), Ribbon Race, and Horse Races. There were trained horses, a flag drill and a square dance."

August 23, 1922

U.S. senator Thomas Sterling introduces S.3935, which seeks "the prevention of willful obstruction of the movement of trains in interstate commerce," as reported in *The Constructor*, the annual publication of the Associated General Contractors. The bill was forwarded to the Senate Committee on Interstate Commerce.

August 24, 1956

A two-vehicle accident north of Wall kills nine people. Five of six family members died in one vehicle, while four young men enrolled at the University of South Dakota were killed in the second vehicle. Although both groups had different destinations, they were on their way to separate weddings.

August 25, 1938

Newly married Bennie and Stella Dickson rob a bank in Elkton, taking a sum of $2,174. A little over two months later, on October 31, they robbed a Brookings bank, stealing a total of $47,233 in cash and bonds.

August 26, 1964

In a memorandum, the U.S. Bureau of Reclamation transfers the management of recreation areas associated with the James Diversion Dam project to the South Dakota Department of Fish and Parks once the project is completed. The department would then oversee a ten-acre recreation area, which included boat ramps and a picnic area. Although Huron used the reservoir created by the dam as a source for the city's water supply for many years, the City of Huron now gets its water from the Missouri River through the Mid-Dakota Rural Water Project.

August 27, 1916

The Fourth South Dakota Infantry band performs its first concert while stationed at San Benito, Texas. After a successful initial performance, a regularly scheduled concert schedule featured the South Dakota band on Sunday evenings.

August 28, 1964

Democratic presidential candidate Lyndon Johnson selects Hubert Humphrey to be his vice presidential running mate. Humphrey, a U.S. senator for Minnesota, was born in Wallace and attended school in Doland.

August 29, 1924

Doane Robinson, superintendent of the State Department of History, writes his first letter to Gutzon Borglum inquiring about his interest in doing a large sculpture in the Black Hills. Robinson's short letter simply stated:

> *In the vicinity of Harney Peak, in the Black Hills of South Dakota are opportunities for heroic sculpture of unusual character. Would it be possible for you to design and supervise a massive sculpture there*[?] *The proposal*

> *has not passed beyond the mere suggestion, but if it be possible for you to undertake the matter I feel quite sure we could arrange to finance such an enterprise. I should be glad to hear from you at your convenience.*

Originally, Robinson proposed a series of sculptures of historic figures along the Needles Highway in the southern Black Hills. Borglum, however, proposed a sculpture that would become Mount Rushmore.

August 30, 1936

President Franklin D. Roosevelt attends the dedication ceremony for Jefferson's image on Mount Rushmore. Roosevelt arrived in Aberdeen two days earlier, on August 28, to tour parts of the state and hold meetings concerning the effects of the drought on South Dakota and other Great Plains states since the early 1930s. When Roosevelt passed through Pierre on his way to the Black Hills, he also visited the nearby Farm Island Civilian Conservation Corps (CCC) project.

August 31, 1896

President Grover Cleveland makes a recess appointment, John Carland to the U.S. District Court for the District of South Dakota. Carland had a prominent legal career dating back to territorial days and was practicing law and living in Sioux Falls at the time of his appointment. As a recess appointee, Carland filled the vacancy in the district court; when the Senate returned from its recess, his appointment was confirmed. In 1911, President William Taft appointed Carland to the U.S. Court of Appeals for the Eighth Circuit, where he served until 1922.

September

As with other months, a variety of events took place in September. The first convention for statehood happened in September. A new college in the northeastern part of the state and a children's museum that is fun for all ages opened. An emotional dedication also took place when thousands of Vietnam veterans visited the state's capital. Just as quickly as summer arrived, fall is now in the air during the "Moon When the Calves Grow Hair."

September 1, 1997

Any surface gold mines not meeting the five-hundred-acre reclamation state law requirement by this date would face a moratorium on new permits. The deadline coincided with codified law 45-6-67.1, which states that "final reclamation shall be completed within three years after all mining under the license has ceased operation, unless such period is extended by the Board of Minerals and Environment."

September 2, 1997

A South Dakota Legislative Research Memorandum reports that the five counties with the highest unemployment rates are Dewey, Shannon, Ziebach, Corson and Buffalo. Each of the counties is included among some of the most economically depressed Sioux reservations located in the state.

September 3, 2014

As part of the state's quasquicentennial events, a wagon train leaves Yankton and heads for Pierre. The trip is expected to take seventeen days.

September 4, 1883

The first constitutional convention for a desired state from the southern part of Dakota Territory is held in Sioux Falls. Over the next two weeks, the convention attendees drafted a constitution, although the gathering had no official authority from the federal government to do so.

September 5, 1986

The Dakota, Minnesota & Eastern Railroad begins operations in South Dakota. When the Chicago & North Western Railway decided to abandon much of its operations in the state in 1985, U.S. senator Larry Pressler opposed the decision. As a result, the Chicago & North Western's situation led to the organization of the Dakota, Minnesota & Eastern Railroad the following year and its eventual acquisition of over one thousand miles of lines, most of which came from the Chicago & North Western.

September 6–7, 1959

Harding County residents observe the county's fiftieth anniversary. The territorial legislature created Harding County in 1881, naming it in honor of Dr. John Harding, who served as the legislature's Speaker of the House that year. It later became a part of neighboring Butte County until the two counties were once again separated in 1909. Harding County then assumed its original name.

September 8, 1919

President Woodrow Wilson stops in Sioux Falls as part of a national speaking tour to gain support for his proposed League of Nations. Because of opposition to the idea of the United States being involved in such an international organization, the U.S. Senate did not ratify the 1919 Versailles Treaty, and the United States did not join the League of Nations, despite its being Wilson's idea.

September 9, 1902

The Northern Normal and Industrial School, now Northern State University, opens. In 1901, the state legislature passed an act stating that "the object and purpose of said school shall be to give instruction to persons of both sexes in manual training and the science and art of teaching, also in the industrial and mechanical trades, arts and sciences, and the allied branches of learning."

September 10, 2010

The U.S. Department of Agriculture Crop Production report forecasts 630.8 million bushels of corn will be harvested in the state, making it the second-largest corn harvest in state history behind the 2009 harvest. The 2010 forecast fell short, as South Dakota farmers harvested 569.7 million bushels of corn.

September 11, 2000

After 125 years of mining gold, the Homestake Mining Company announces that it is closing at the end of 2001. During its existence, the mine produced nearly forty million ounces of gold.

September 12, 2010

The Children's Museum in Brookings officially opens, with exhibits featuring science, history, art and literature. On the museum's fifth anniversary, Governor Dennis Daugaard declared September 12, 2015, "Children's Museum of South Dakota Day." According to the governor's proclamation, the Children's Museum had already entertained visitors from all fifty states and numerous countries in its first five years.

September 13, 1970

The record for Rapid City's earliest snowfall since 1888 is broken by two days. The 1970 record stands until September 11, 2014, when an inch of snow fell in the city.

September 14, 1963

The Fischer Quints, four girls and a boy, of Aberdeen become the first known surviving quintuplets born in the United States. Although the family received a great deal of media attention, they eventually elected to have a more private, personal lifestyle.

September 15

1966

U.S. secretary of state Dean Rusk gives the address dedicating the Big Bend Dam, the last of the Pick-Sloan Missouri River dams to be built in South Dakota.

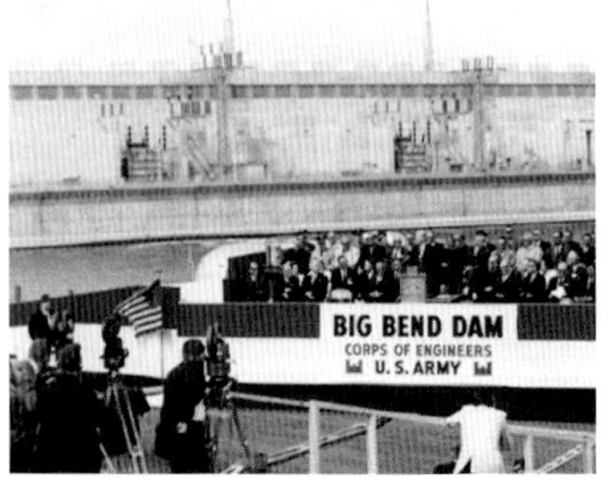

Big Bend Dam dedication. *Senator George McGovern Collection, Dakota Wesleyan University Archives, Mitchell, South Dakota.*

1982

Eureka native Al Neuharth publishes the first edition of his newspaper, *USA Today*. In addition to being the founder of *USA Today*, Neuharth contributed a great deal to journalism, including the Freedom Forum and the Newseum in Washington, D.C.

2001

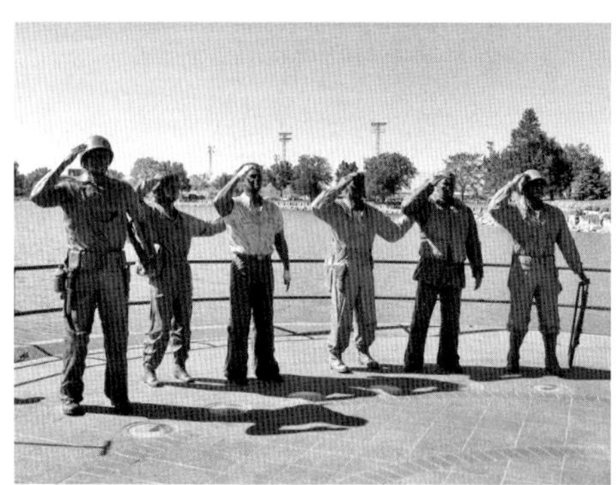

World War II Memorial. *Brad Tennant.*

South Dakota dedicates its World War II Memorial. The site features six bronze figures representing the various branches served by South Dakota military personnel. According to the artist statement, the figures represent a marine, a sailor, a pilot, an army GI, a representative of the Coast Guard and Merchant Marines and a female nurse representing the women who served in the Women's Army Corps (WACS), the Navy's Women Accepted for Volunteer Emergency Service (WAVES) and the Coast Guard Women's Reserve (SPARS, the acronym for the Coast Guard's motto "Semper Paratus—Always Ready").

September 16, 2006

More than 32,000 people attend the dedication of the South Dakota Vietnam War Memorial in Pierre. The memorial features a seven-foot-tall soldier carrying the dog tags of a fellow soldier who was killed in action. Artists Lee Leuning and Sherri Treeby designed the memorial sculpture, which recognizes the more than 28,000 South Dakotans who served during the Vietnam era and the 207 South Dakotans who lost their lives during their service.

September 17, 1937

Abraham Lincoln's image on Mount Rushmore is dedicated.

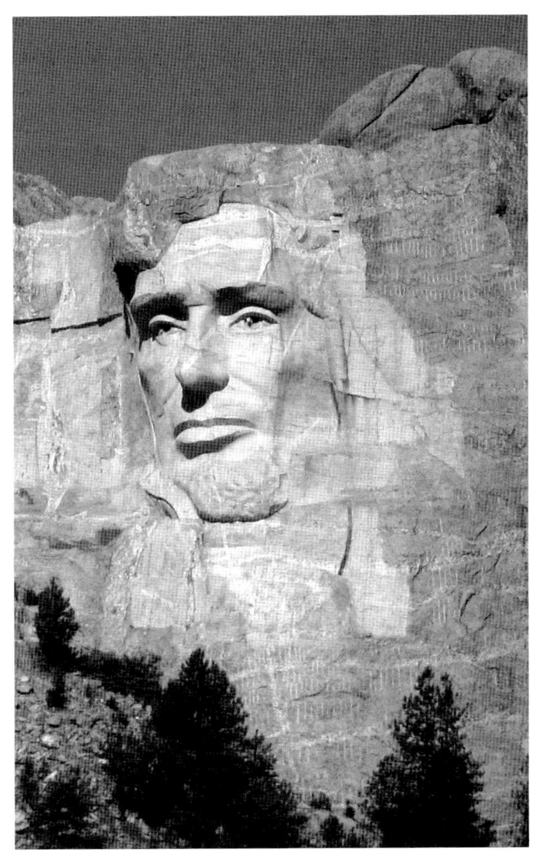

Abraham Lincoln, Mount Rushmore. *Brad Tennant.*

September 18, 1961

The South Dakota School for the Blind begins classes at its new campus in Aberdeen. Gary had been the site of the school since its beginning in 1900, but the South Dakota legislature decided in 1959 to relocate the facility to Aberdeen. Today, the school for the blind is known as the South Dakota School for the Visually Handicapped.

September 19, 1989

President George H.W. Bush stops in Sioux Falls for a little over ninety minutes to recognize South Dakota's statehood centennial. During his short visit, Bush planted a "centennial" tree at Terrace Park to honor South Dakota's first one hundred years.

September 20, 1946

The 175th Fighter Squadron of the newly created South Dakota Air National Guard receives federal recognition. On July 10, 1946, Medal of Honor recipient and Marine ace Joe Foss was appointed to form an Air National Guard squadron at Sioux Falls. The 175th Fighter Squadron's original mission focused on a means of defense against possible airborne weapons. Today, the Joe Foss Field Air National Guard Station serves as the home base for the South Dakota Air National Guard's 114th Fighter Wing.

September 21, 1972

A public hearing is held near the South Dakota–Wyoming state line concerning the construction of Interstate 90 and a Draft Environmental Impact Statement. Interstate 90 from Spearfish to Wyoming was the last segment to be completed in South Dakota. The South Dakota portion of the interstate, which runs about 413 miles in an east–west direction through the southern part of the state, was completed in 1976.

September 22, 2000

After four generations of the Waltner family overseeing the functions of the First National Bank in Freeman, CorTrust Bank assumes business operations. Members of the Waltner family had been involved in the bank for ninety-eight years, dating to the institution's beginning in 1902.

September 23, 1918

South Dakota officials report the first cases of the Spanish influenza in the state. By mid-October, the influenza reached pandemic proportions. In the first week of November, 218 deaths were attributed to influenza across the state, and by the end of the year, influenza accounted for over 1,800 deaths statewide.

September 24, 1946

The Sisseton-Wahpeton Sioux Tribe of the Sisseton-Wahpeton Lake Traverse Sioux Reservation approves its constitution by a vote of 300 for and 146 against. The preamble to the constitution of the Sisseton-Wahpeton Oyate simply states, "We, the Sisseton-Wahpeton Sioux Tribe, in order to form a tribal government for the proper exercise of our tribal rights and responsibilities, do establish this Constitution and By-laws."

September 25, 2012

The South Dakota Housing for the Homeless Consortium releases its summer 2012 survey and count of those identified as homeless. According to the consortium, the number of homeless individuals is 1,166. The consortium began its homeless counts in 2009.

September 26, 1919

A dance is held as a fundraiser for American Legion Sully Post 79 in Onida. Money from the dance was the first to be raised to go toward the new post.

September 27, 1927

About five hundred Ku Klux Klan members participate in a march and rally in downtown Sioux Falls. Although the KKK is known for its racism and anti-Semitism, many of the KKK gatherings throughout South Dakota were anti-Catholic in nature.

September 28

1892

The first Corn Palace in Mitchell opens to the public. This begins a community-wide ten-day celebration highlighting the new structure and its Corn Belt Exposition. Although the main purpose of the Corn Palace was to promote South Dakota's agricultural potential, today, approximately a half million visitors stop to view the beautifully designed murals that are featured each year at the "World's Only Corn Palace."

1931

The Yankton Sioux Tribe approves its constitution. Whereas most of the other Sioux tribes located within South Dakota ratified their constitutions after receiving authorization from the Indian Reorganization Act of 1934, the Yankton Sioux Tribe approved its constitution several years before Congress passed the IRA.

September 29, 1986

Hundreds of farmers representing the American Agricultural Movement, the Farmers Union and the National Farmers Organization gather in Sioux Falls to protest President Ronald Reagan's agricultural policies. Reagan addressed the sizeable crowd at the Sioux Falls Arena and, afterward, invited two of the spokesmen for the farmers to visit with him as he rode to the airport.

September 30, 2008

A nonprofit organization reports that 1,444 children are in the state's foster care program on this date. Other sources state that there were 1,311 children in foster care in South Dakota during the month of September 2008.

October

October means pheasant hunting and the arrival of hunters to the state from around the country, but the first pheasant-hunting season lasted only one day. October is the "Moon of the Changing Season." Although snow in October is common, one early-season blizzard resulted in livestock losses in the tens of thousands. The state acknowledged that Columbus does not deserve a holiday, and the president welcomed home troops from the Spanish-American War. Plus, a South Dakotan won gold in the Olympics.

October 1, 1889

In preparation for statehood, voters in what would soon be South Dakota approve the state seal design and description, as well as the 1889 state constitution.

October 2, 1965

The South Dakota Park and Recreation Association is founded. The SDPRA states that its mission is "to promote the growth, status and unity of all phases of parks, recreation, and leisure services in the state of South Dakota."

October 3, 1890

Dr. Daniel Royer, the newly appointed Pine Ridge Indian agent, receives instructions to stop the Ghost Dance. Royer, who knew little about any American Indian cultures, let alone that of the Lakota, was appointed to the position as a political favor from U.S. senator Richard Pettigrew. In addition to his ignorance, Royer's communications to authorities in Washington, D.C., reflected a growing paranoia about the people of the Pine Ridge Agency.

October 4

1927

Gutzon Borglum begins carving on Mount Rushmore.

2013

Winter storm Atlas hits the northern plains, affecting the western part of South Dakota. Although seasonal temperatures in the seventies and eighties were recorded in the days before the storm, Atlas dumped several feet of snow over the next few days. The storm began on October 3, when rain turned to freezing rain and then snow. On October 4, heavy, wet snow accumulated while wind gusts ranged from fifty to seventy miles per hour. Extensive damage occurred to buildings, trees and power lines. In addition, estimates of losses of livestock, including cattle, sheep and horses, were initially placed as high as seventy thousand; many residents called Atlas the "Cattlemen's Blizzard." Due to the storm's concentration in western South Dakota, little national media reported the severity of the event, causing many to refer to it as the "Forgotten Blizzard."

October 5, 1935

By a vote of 123 to 42, eligible tribal members ratify the constitution of the Lower Brule Sioux Tribe, as allowed by the 1934 Indian Reorganization Act.

October 6, 1900

John Brennan, Pine Ridge Indian agent, receives orders to collect a $1 tax on "excess cattle" on the reservation. Some non-Indian ranchers freely grazed large herds on the reservation ranges under the pretense that the cattle would be sold to the Pine Ridge Oglala Lakota. According to the provisions of the tax, herds with less than one hundred head would be exempt; however, herds in excess of one hundred head would be taxed $1 for every head over the limit. Revenue from the tax totaled $2,241 during its first five months of implementation. Brennan later estimated that, as a result of the new tax, nearly three thousand head had been sold by the end of 1904 to avoid paying the fee.

October 7, 1907

Two trains collide head-on in the Chicago, Milwaukee & St. Paul rail yard at Mitchell. An engineer and a fireman died in the accident.

October 8, 1990

South Dakota replaces Columbus Day with Native American Day as part of its "Year of Reconciliation" marking the one hundredth anniversary of the December 1890 Wounded Knee Massacre.

October 9, 1942

Captain Joe Foss and his unit land at Henderson Field at Guadalcanal, Solomon Islands. Foss's unit, known as "Joe's Flying Circus," was instrumental in protecting Guadalcanal during the next several months.

October 10, 2014

The University of South Dakota celebrates its one hundredth Dakota Days homecoming festivities. When begun in 1914, the event was called "South Dakota Day," but the weeklong celebration for students and alumni is now called simply "Dakota Days" or "D-Days."

October 11, 1924

The Meridian Bridge at Yankton is dedicated, permitting traffic to cross between South Dakota and Nebraska. Originally, the two-tiered Missouri River bridge was a toll bridge, but tolls were discontinued in 1953. Eighty-four years after the Meridian Bridge dedication, the new Discovery Bridge was dedicated on October 11, 2008. Today, the Meridian Bridge is used as a bike and pedestrian span.

October 12, 1991

Arlette Schweitzer gives birth to her grandchildren. When it was determined that her daughter could not give birth, Schweitzer opted to have embryos from her daughter and son-in-law implanted into her womb, which she then carried to full term. She gave birth to twins—a boy and a girl.

October 13, 1983

WEB Water awards the contract for the construction of an intake and pumping plant to be located south of Mobridge. Construction began one week after the contract was awarded. The "WEB" acronym is formed from Walworth, Edmunds and Brown Counties, but the water pipeline now serves residents in fourteen counties in South Dakota and three in North Dakota.

October 14

1899

President William McKinley addresses a large crowd as part of the "Welcome Home" celebration for members of the First Regiment, South Dakota Volunteers after their return from service in the Spanish-American War. Estimates place the crowds for the parade and McKinley's address at 100,000 people. McKinley's trip marked the first time that a president visited South Dakota.

1964

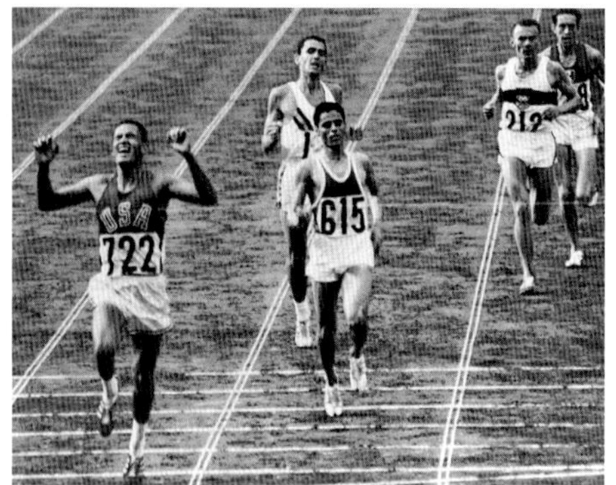

Billy Mills wins gold in Tokyo. *Public domain as a work of the U.S. Marine Corps.*

Billy Mills, an Oglala Lakota from the Pine Ridge Indian Reservation, wins the 10,000-meter run at the Tokyo Olympic Games and becomes the first and only American athlete to win an Olympic gold medal in that event. In 2012, President Obama awarded Mills the Presidential Citizens Medal for his nonprofit organization Running Strong for American Indian Youth.

October 15, 1966

Mount Rushmore is listed in the National Register of Historic Places. Today, the "Shrine of Democracy" receives more than two million visitors per year and is listed as the Mount Rushmore National Memorial Historic District.

October 16, 1979

The Royal Swedish Academy of Sciences announces that Dr. Theodore W. Schultz of the University of Chicago is one of two recipients of the Nobel Prize in Economic Sciences. The academy recognized Schultz, who was born in Arlington in 1902, for his seminal research involving the economic development and challenges of developing countries.

October 17, 1933

The Civilian Conservation Corps camp named "Lightning Creek" opens in the Black Hills a few miles from Jewel Cave. As with many of the CCC camps, work included building dams and thinning forested areas.

October 18, 1995

A WSR-88D (Doppler) radar is commissioned for the Sioux Falls National Weather Service. The National Weather Service heralded the new weather surveillance radar (WSR) as "another milestone" in Doppler radar.

October 19, 1893

Regular passenger and freight service begins on the Sioux Falls, Yankton & Southwestern Railroad line, administered by the Great Northern Railway. This line connected Yankton to Sioux Falls, which could now be traveled in less than three hours.

October 20, 1940

The dedication ceremony for the CCC-constructed dam and Sheridan Lake draws a large crowd numbering around five thousand. The dam was the largest earthen dam created by the Civilian Conservation Corps in South Dakota, and Sheridan Lake became one of the largest lakes in the Black Hills.

October 21–23, 1911

President William Howard Taft arrives in Rapid City to begin the first day of a three-day visit to South Dakota. Taft gave a number of speeches in which he addressed international concerns over peace. Traveling by train, Taft addressed crowds in several Black Hills communities before going to Pierre, Huron and Aberdeen.

October 24, 2000

Representative John Thune introduces H.R.5528, "a bill to provide housing assistance to Native American Indians and Native Hawaiians, to promote home ownership in Indian reservations, to promote employment in Indian reservations." The bill was approved and signed into law in late December.

October 25, 1999

Professional golfer Payne Stewart's plane crashes near Mina. Along with Stewart, two pilots and three other passengers died when the Learjet 35 aircraft crashed. The National Transportation Safety Board determined that the loss of cabin pressure incapacitated the pilots. The original flight plan stated that the aircraft left Orlando, Florida, for Dallas, Texas; however, the jet veered off course, heading north until it ran out of fuel and crashed.

October 26, 1926

John Philip Sousa conducts his band as it performs on the University of South Dakota campus. The concert took place in the university's year-old assembly hall; in 1929, it became known as Slagle Auditorium. Today, it is known as the Bailey and Kathy Aalfs Auditorium in Slagle Hall.

October 27, 1910

Attendees at a meeting in Aberdeen formally establish the South Dakota Good Roads Association, with A.E. Chamberlain of Brookings County elected to be the association's first president. The idea of a good roads association began with J.W. Parmley of Ipswich as early as 1907. Parmley eventually became the South Dakota Good Roads Association's president.

October 28, 1999

Nine years after governor George S. Mickelson declared 1990 a "Year of Reconciliation" among the state's Indian and non-Indian populations, U.S. senator Ben Nighthorse Campbell of Colorado shares with the Senate a story of a situation in which an announcement declared an "Indian Hunting Season" in South Dakota. The racist flyer reflected bigotry at its worse, as the person responsible used a number of racial epithets. Campbell used the material to denounce hatred against "any American—red, black, white, or yellow" and encouraged his senate colleagues to do the same.

October 29, 1967

The Gary Historical Association assumes responsibility for the community buffalo supper. The Methodist Men previously served the meal, but the event became too large for them to handle. Information from the Gary Historical Association says that, over the years, the dinner drew as many as one thousand people, although seating was limited to two hundred at a time. A typical menu included "roast buffalo, mashed potatoes, gravy, corn, cranberry relish, milk, coffee, relish plate and assorted breads" and dessert.

October 30, 1919

South Dakota opens its first official pheasant-hunting season, which was one day only. The Chinese ringneck pheasant, which is now the official state bird, is not native to South Dakota. Although attempts to introduce pheasants to the state occurred as early as 1898, the first sustainable pheasant population began in 1908, when pheasants were released in Spink County. Today, the state's pheasant-hunting season annually draws hunters from all over the United States.

October 31, 1941

Carving on Mount Rushmore is declared completed after fourteen years of work, and the monument is formally dedicated.

November

November is the "Moon of Falling Leaves." Winter is approaching, as is evident by the migration of waterfowl, the lower temperatures, occasional snowfalls and the bare trees that have shed their leaves. November marks the beginning of South Dakota as a state. It is also the month of elections; over the years, there have been a number of significant elections that impacted South Dakota at the state and national levels. Two Hutterite men died as martyrs for their pacifist beliefs during World War I, while Lakota, Dakota and Nakota code talkers were recognized for their service in World War II.

November 1, 1989

Deadwood begins legalized gambling after state voters approved a Constitutional amendment in the 1988 election.

November 2

1889

South Dakota receives statehood after President Benjamin Harrison signed two proclamations making both North and South Dakota states. To avoid any jealousy, Harrison had the documents shuffled and the top portions covered so that even he did not know which state was admitted first. Harrison reportedly stated that "they were born together. They are one, and I will make them twins." North Dakota, however, is listed as the thirty-ninth state, and South Dakota is the fortieth state, based on alphabetical order. The two individuals who represent South Dakota in the National Statuary Hall in the U.S. Capitol both played important roles in the statehood movement. William H.H. Beadle was an early advocate for a separate state in the southern part of Dakota Territory, and the Reverend Joseph Ward is credited with the state motto "Under God the people rule."

An Original Autograph Telegram sent to the Governors of North Dakota and South Dakota notifying them of The Admission of the two states into the Union in November 2, 1889 by Secretary of State James G. Blaine.

The last Act in the admission of the two Dakotas in the union was completed at the White House at three o'clock and forty minutes this afternoon by the President Benjamin Harrison signing at that moment the two states.

The article on Prohibition submitted separately in each state was adopted in both. The article providing for minority representation in South Dakota was rejected by the people.

This is the first instance in the history of the National Government of twin states. North and South Dakota entered the Union at same moment.

James G. Blaine

James Blaine statehood telegraph transcription. *South Dakota State Historical Society.*

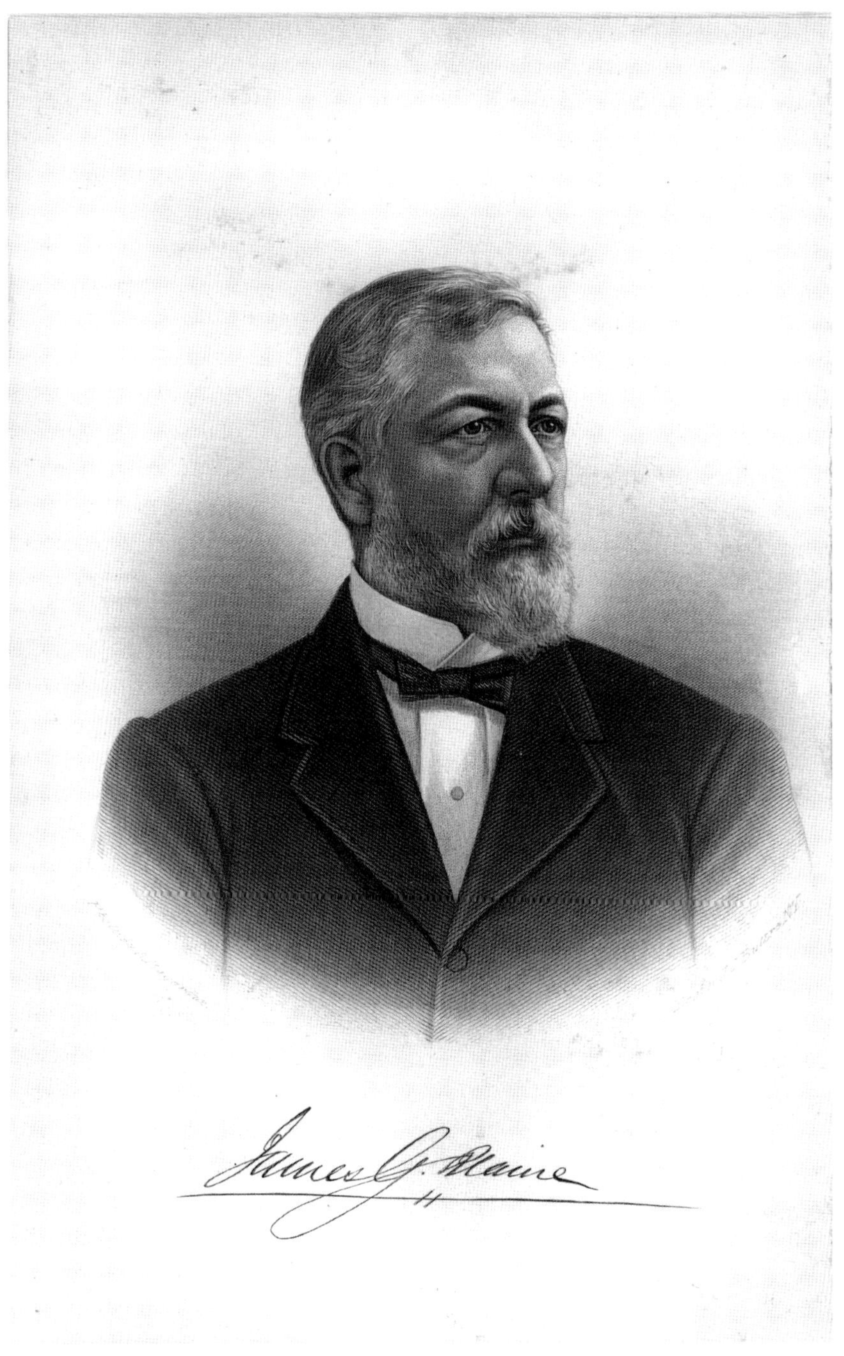

Secretary of State James Blaine. *South Dakota State Historical Society.*

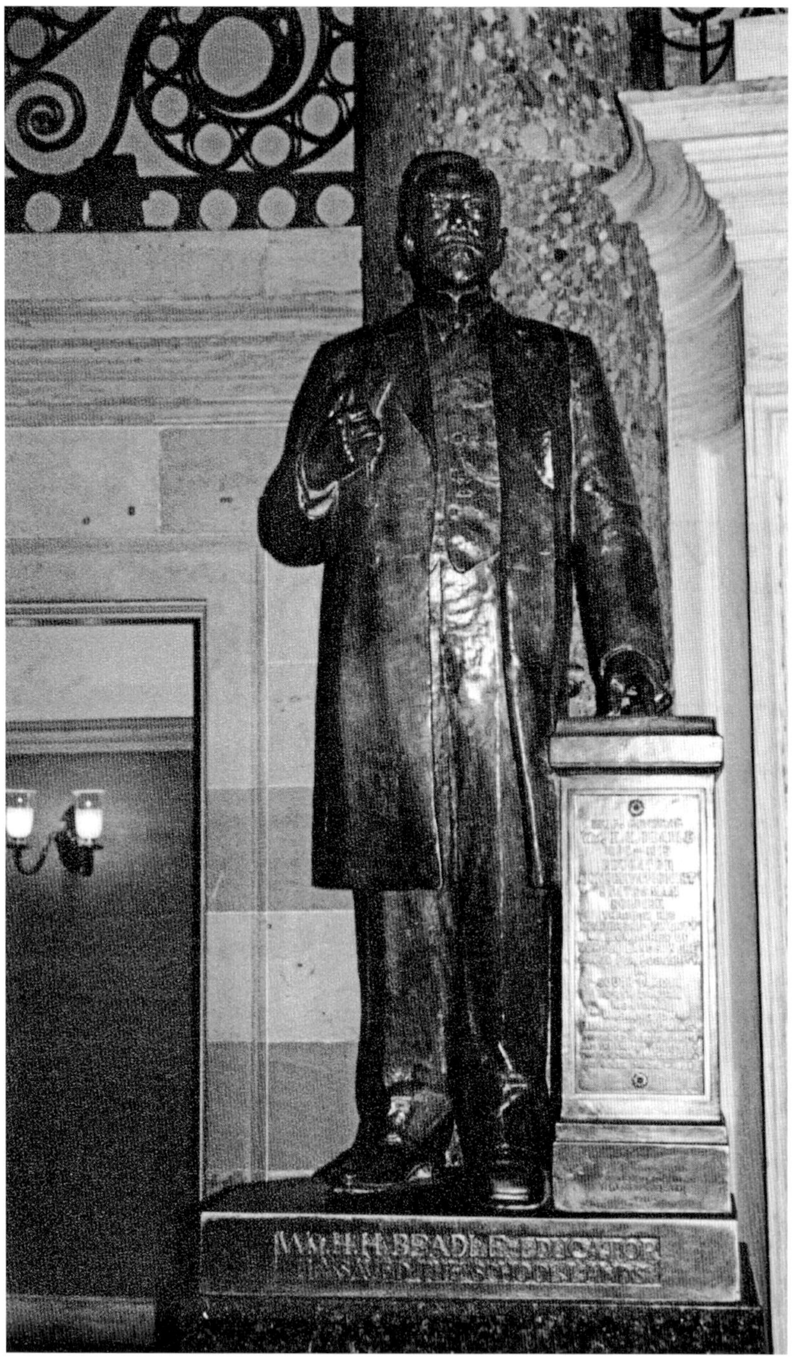

William H.H. Beadle, National Statuary Hall. *Brad Tennant*.

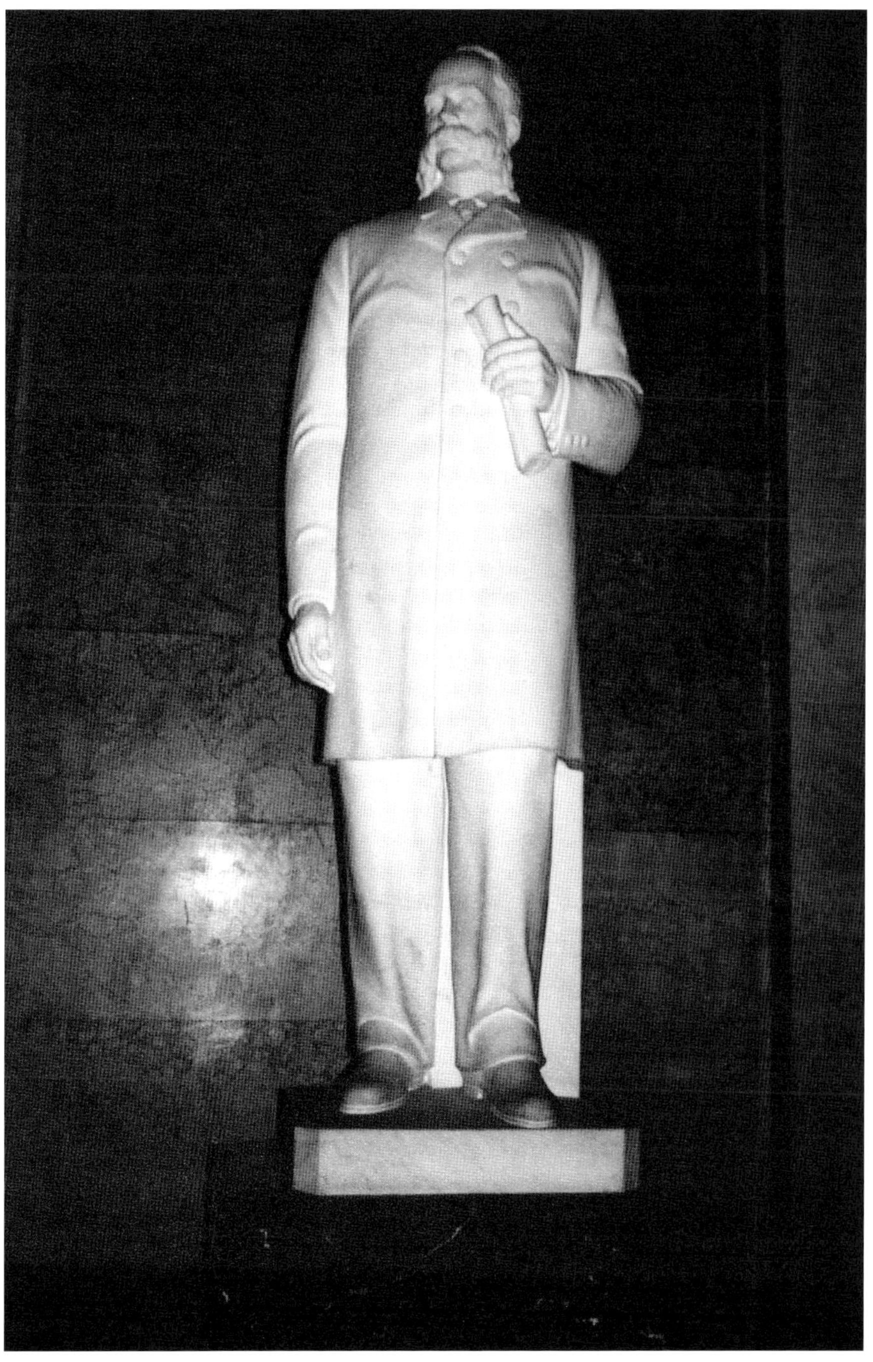

Reverend Joseph Ward, National Statuary Hall. *Brad Tennant.*

2014

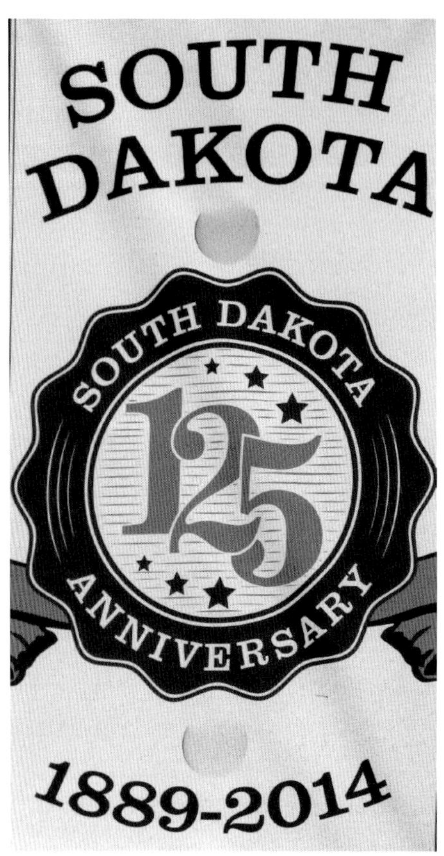

South Dakota quasquicentennial banner. *Brad Tennant.*

South Dakota celebrates its quasquicentennial—125 years of statehood.

November 3

1896

Supported by South Dakota Populists, Democratic presidential candidate William Jennings Bryan receives the state's four electoral votes over Republican William McKinley.

1936

As in the 1932 election, South Dakota's electoral votes go to Democratic presidential candidate Franklin D. Roosevelt in hopes that FDR's New Deal programs will provide the relief, recovery and reform measures needed during the Great Depression.

1964

For only the fourth time in state history, South Dakota voters choose a Democratic presidential candidate, supporting Lyndon Baines Johnson over Republican Barry Goldwater.

November 4, 1902

Incumbent governor Charles Herreid wins reelection in a gubernatorial election that featured candidates from four different political parties: the Republican, Democratic, Socialist and Prohibition Parties.

November 5

1898

South Dakota voters approve the use of the initiative and referendum, making South Dakota the first state to allow for such forms of direct democracy. The Populist Party, and specifically Father Robert Haire, promoted the initiative and referendum as a means of direct democracy in which the people would have the means to more effectively deal with issues affecting farmers and the state's rural communities.

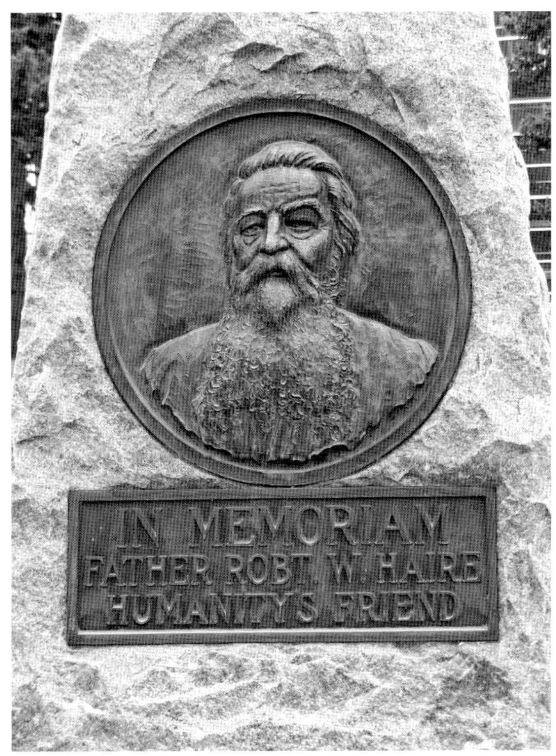

Father Robert Haire Memorial. *Brad Tennant.*

1918

South Dakota voters approve a state constitutional amendment giving women the right to vote. Six previous attempts to approve women's suffrage, including an 1894 ballot measure that would have allowed women's suffrage in school elections, failed. The 1918 constitutional amendment pertaining to women's suffrage passed with 49,318 "yes" and 28,934 "no" votes.

November 6, 1915

A complaint is filed against the Onida Telephone Company for what was considered insufficient nighttime and Sunday telephone service.

November 7, 1972

Not only did U.S. senator George McGovern lose his presidential election bid to Republican incumbent Richard Nixon, but McGovern also did not win his home state. Nixon received 166,476 popular votes in the state, and McGovern received 139,945. All four of the state's electoral votes then went to Nixon.

November 8

1932

With the Great Depression well underway, Democratic presidential candidate Franklin D. Roosevelt receives South Dakota's electoral votes. This was only the second time in the state's history that the voters supported a democratic presidential candidate. After facing severe economic conditions since the early 1920s, farmers and rural communities turned to FDR and the Democratic Party in hopes of positive changes.

1938

Gladys Pyle wins a special election to complete the last two months of the term of South Dakota's late U.S. senator Peter Norbeck, thus making her the first woman to be elected to that office from South Dakota.

Although Pyle won the special election to replace Norbeck, Chandler Gurney appeared on the regular 1938 ballot and won the senate race for the Seventy-Sixth Congress, scheduled to start in January 1939. Since Congress did not convene until January 3, 1939, Pyle was never officially sworn into the Senate.

1956

Strato-Lab I, under the command of Malcolm Ross and M.L. Lewis, casts off from the Stratobowl. The *Strato-Lab* flight reached a world-record altitude for a manned balloon of seventy-six thousand feet, breaking the 1935 *Explorer II* record.

1989

Winds reaching sixty miles an hour blow thousands of tumbleweeds into Mobridge. Recent dry conditions led to an abundance of Russian thistles along the Missouri River. The plants typically die in late summer and early fall, when the wind snaps them off near ground-level, allowing them to tumble. The town spent $8,500 to remove the estimated thirty tons of tumbleweeds.

November 9, 1992

The revised state flag is officially adopted. The nickname appearing on the new design was changed from "The Sunshine State" to "The Mount Rushmore State."

November 10, 1978

Badlands National Monument is re-designated, from monument status to a national park.

November 11

1933

A large dust storm, or black blizzard, affects much of the state as high winds carry the topsoil for miles.

1935

U.S. Army Air Corps captains Orvil A. Anderson and Albert W. Stevens reach a record altitude of 72,395 feet in a pressurized gondola with a helium-filled balloon called *Explorer II*. It not only exceeded the altitude record established the previous year by *Explorer I*, but it also included a variety of instruments to gather scientific information. *Explorer II*'s flight lasted slightly over eight hours and covered approximately 225 miles before landing near White Lake. As with *Explorer I*, the National Geographic Society co-sponsored the flight with the Army Air Corps.

November 12, 1924

The bridge spanning the Missouri River at Mobridge is formally dedicated. This is the first toll-free, permanent wagon/automobile bridge across the Missouri River and the first of five planned highway bridges to be constructed in South Dakota during the 1920s. Approximately ten thousand people attended the formal ceremony, creating an impressive procession as they crossed the bridge.

November 13, 1903

The Aberdeen *Democrat* newspaper reports on a recent meeting of the Social Science Club. The article reported that "the race problem under discussion was that of the negro and how best to avoid or remedy the evils now resulting from the presence in this country of many millions of people of African descent." After the speaker and club members discussed the topic, the speaker concluded that he "was more inclined to look hopefully to the assimilation of the race through benign influences of education, religion and thrift."

November 14, 1963

As fear of a possible nuclear war increases, the University of South Dakota publishes *A Civil Defense In-Shelter Guide for University of South Dakota*.

November 15, 1955

The consolidation of the city of Sioux Falls with South Sioux Falls is viewed favorably by voters. In Sioux Falls, voters approved the consolidation on this date by a vote of 2,714 for the measure and 450 against. Previously, on October 18, 1955, South Sioux Falls voters cast their support by a vote of 704 to 227.

November 16, 1998

The Make-A-Wish South Dakota program grants its 300th wish. Make-A-Wish began in South Dakota in 1984 and has provided "special wishes" for children with medical conditions since then.

November 17, 1973

Allen, James and David Fryer of Sioux Falls brutally attack five South Dakota teenagers at the Gitchie Manitou State Preserve in Iowa. The victims ranged in age from thirteen to eighteen. The brothers murdered the four boys and raped a young girl, who later identified the assailants. Upon being convicted, the Fryers received life sentences without parole.

November 18, 2004

The *Congressional Record* for the U.S. Senate includes a resolution from the Farmers Union titled "A Resolution Commemorating 26 Years of Service By United States Senator Thomas A. Daschle." John Thune defeated Daschle, a Democrat and the incumbent senator, in the November 2 election.

November 19, 1918

Four men from the Rockport Hutterite Colony near Alexandria arrive at the Fort Leavenworth military prison after being transferred from Alcatraz. Brothers Joseph, Michael and David Hofer and brother-in-law Jacob Wipf were drafted into military service; however, as members of the Hutterite faith, they were pacifists and conscientious objectors. As a result of their disobeying military orders, they were originally sentenced to twenty years at the Alcatraz military prison. After suffering various forms of torture, the military transferred the men to the Fort Leavenworth prison, where Joseph died on November 29, 1918. Michael died three days later, on December 2, 1918. The brothers are buried in the Rockport Colony cemetery with "MARTYR" written on their grave markers. Since Hutterites speak a German dialect, they faced a great deal of resentment during World War I. As a result of the discrimination and prejudice they suffered, all but the Bon Homme Hutterite Colony left the state and moved to Canada. It was not until the Depression years of the 1930s that the state attempted to make amends and invite colonies to return to South Dakota.

November 20, 2013

Lakota, Dakota and Nakota code talkers who served in World War II against Germany and Japan posthumously receive the Congressional Code Talkers Medal for their service. Sixty-nine code talkers representing eight of the Sioux Nation tribes located within the state were recognized during a ceremony held at the U.S. Capitol.

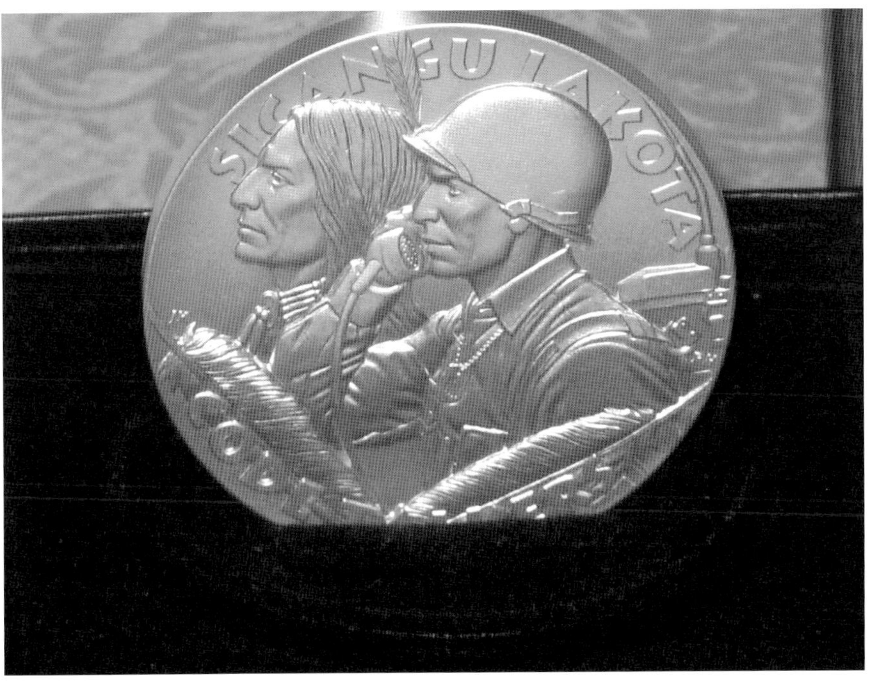

Congressional Code Talker Medal presented to Noah Whitebird Sr. *Brad Tennant.*

November 21, 1963

Contracts exceeding a little over $1.16 million are awarded for a new Student Union Building on the campus of the University of South Dakota.

November 22, 2002

Justice Judith Meierhenry is sworn in, becoming the first woman on the South Dakota Supreme Court. Governor William Janklow appointed Meierhenry earlier in the month to become the newest justice of the five-member Supreme Court.

November 23, 1935

Members of the Rosebud Sioux Tribe of the Rosebud Reservation voted to approve its constitution by a vote of 992 to 643. As with the other federally recognized tribes in the state, the ratification of a tribal constitution resulted from the Indian Reorganization Act, also commonly known as the Wheeler-Howard Act.

November 24, 1975

American Indian activist Anna Mae Aquash, who had been extradited to South Dakota from Oregon and was facing charges of illegal transportation of firearms and explosives, flees once again after being released on bail. The following February, her decomposing body was found by a rancher. An autopsy showed that she had been shot at the base of her skull at close range. A lengthy investigation resulted in murder charges being brought against individuals associated with the American Indian Movement, who believed that Aquash had acted as a spy for the federal government against AIM leadership.

November 25, 1922

WNAX radio begins broadcasting from Yankton. In May, the Dakota Radio Apparatus Company had been established, and in early November, the company received a license from the U.S. Department of Commerce allowing the station to begin broadcasting. WNAX's first broadcast consisted of providing music to area listeners, which included those within about a forty-mile radius of Yankton.

November 26, 2015

For the sixth consecutive year, the Macy's Thanksgiving Day Parade in New York City includes an entry representing South Dakota and, more specifically, Mount Rushmore. The South Dakota float featured a replica of Mount Rushmore as well as mascots portraying Washington, Jefferson, Roosevelt and Lincoln and the Christian band MercyMe.

November 27–28, 2005

An ice storm causes excessive damage to twelve hundred transmission poles and approximately 725 miles of power lines maintained by the East River Electric Power Cooperative. Freezing rain quickly accumulated on the lines, and when wind gusts reached speeds of fifty miles an hour, the weight of the ice caused the transmission poles to break, downing lines over a wide region in the eastern part of the state.

November 27, 1964

A press release from the U.S. Fish and Wildlife Service identifies the black-footed ferret as facing extinction in South Dakota as well as in North Dakota and Nebraska.

November 28

1902

The Aberdeen *Democrat* reports that the "cold but pleasant weather" provides good conditions for ice boating at Sand Lake. During ideal conditions, a number of ice boats can now be found sailing on the lake.

2013

Joan Jett is replaced on the South Dakota float for the Macy's Thanksgiving Day Parade. Ranchers criticized her being on the float because she is an avid supporter of People for the Ethical Treatment of Animals.

South Dakota

Minuteman Missile National Historic Site

An Opportunity For Preservation

Broaden your perspective of the word "park" from a recreation site to the larger dictionary definition: *"a place set aside for people."* The National Park System includes nearly 380 areas, only 67 of which carry the title "National Park." The agency also caretakes "National Military Parks," "National Historic Sites," National Battlefields," "National Monuments," and other cultural or natural areas. In fact, over 55% of the sites under the jurisdiction of the National Park Service have history or culture as their primary purpose for preservation. Our agency is responsible for protecting our collective pasts for future generations - whether environmental or event based. Ranging from Yosemite to Yellowstone to Gettysburg to the U.S.S. Arizona Memorial, the National Park Service is given responsiblity by Congress for areas of national significance determined to be suitable and feasible for protection.

Minuteman Missile National Historic Site brochure. *Brad Tennant.*

November 29, 1999

President Bill Clinton signs the Minuteman Missile National Historic Site Establishment Act, placing Delta 1 Launch Control Facility and Delta 9 Launch Facility under the National Park System.

November 30, 2015

The abandoned town of Swett is once again listed for sale, at a reduced asking price of $250,000. The town is listed as having about six acres with a couple of abandoned buildings.

December

December, the "Moon of the Popping Trees," is marred by such events as Sitting Bull's death and the country's largest mass shooting. It is also the month when an asylum opened for "insane Indians." December also marked the end of two notable eras in South Dakota history. The state saw the end of a major gold-mining operation that began in the territorial days and the end of one of the longest-running televised children's programs.

December 1, 2000

The Gilt Edge Mine is placed on the Superfund National Priorities List. Reclamation efforts continue to focus on concerns over acid drainage.

December 2, 1957

The U.S. Army conducts biological tests over South Dakota as part of "Operation LAC" (Large Area Coverage). Using what was then considered nontoxic simulants, the project's objective was to determine the impact of biological or chemical agents should they be used in warfare. Although various cities and regions were included in the tests, the first test occurred on this date, when simulants such as zinc cadmium sulfide were sprayed in a swath from South Dakota to International Falls, Minnesota.

December 3, 1942

The Army Administration School at South Dakota State College is established. The purpose of this and other administration schools focused on training individuals as administrative clerks for the Army Air Corps.

December 4

1919

South Dakota becomes the twenty-first state to ratify the Nineteenth Amendment, allowing women's suffrage. In six different state elections, ballot measures giving women the right to vote in South Dakota were all defeated at the polls. The elections of 1890, 1898, 1910, 1914 and 1916 would have allowed women complete suffrage in the state. An 1894 measure, which would have granted women's suffrage in school elections, was also defeated. It was not until the 1918 election that voters approved women's suffrage in South Dakota. The Nineteenth Amendment was ratified on August 18, 1920.

2013

The South Dakota Board on Geographic Names unanimously votes to ask the legislature to revise the state law so that the word *Negro* can remain in place names around the state. The original law mandated that the words *Squaw* and *Negro* be replaced; however, after receiving public input, sentiment felt that the word *Negro* is not offensive.

December 5, 1901

As with many community grain elevators around the state, the Farmers Co-Operative Elevator Company in Hurley files a complaint with the South Dakota Railroad Commission regarding the lack of rail cars for shipping grain. In his complaint, the manager of the Farmers Co-Operative Elevator Company expressed his frustration about the lack of cars available during the fall harvest. Furthermore, due to the shortage, the elevator had been turning away business, as it had no more room for storage.

December 6, 1999

A series of recent unsolved deaths of American Indians leads to a public meeting and forum hosted by the South Dakota Advisory Committee to the U.S. Commission on Civil Rights. The meeting, which was held in Rapid City, included representatives from federal, tribal, state, county and local entities, as well as the general public. The advisory committee oversaw the forum, which was titled "Native Americans and the Administration of Justice in South Dakota."

December 7, 1935

By a vote of 576 to 366, eligible voters ratify the constitution and bylaws of the Cheyenne River Tribe of the Sioux Indians. The 1934 Indian Reorganization Act and later amendments allowed the Cheyenne River Sioux to establish its own tribal constitution.

December 8, 2003

A Moody County jury convicts U.S. representative William Janklow of second-degree manslaughter as a result of a traffic accident in which Janklow struck and killed a motorcyclist at an intersection. Janklow later resigned from his position in Congress. Although his defense argued that Janklow may have been suffering from low blood sugar, the prosecuting attorney noted Janklow's numerous traffic violations for speeding.

December 9, 1936

The drama classes of Eastern State Normal School (now Dakota State University) perform the play *The Command Performance* by C. Stafford Dickens. The college orchestra provided the music for the production.

December 10, 1972

The Rapid City Stake of the Church of Jesus Christ of Latter-day Saints is created. The stake served congregations in ten branches and wards in the Rapid City area.

December 11, 1909

Saloon bartender Bud Stephens shoots and kills Dode McKenzie in the cow town of LeBeau. Dode's father, Murdo McKenzie, a powerful cattleman and manager of the Matador Cattle Company, sought to have Stephens convicted of murder. Stephens, however, claimed that he had been warned that McKenzie was looking for him, so he took the offensive and shot McKenzie first, twice in the chest and twice in the back. A jury trial resulted in Stephens being acquitted.

December 12, 2014

The South Dakota Department of Public Safety decides to discontinue a $100,000 ad campaign for winter driving safety. The ad's slogan, "Don't jerk and drive," faced ridicule throughout the country for its sexual innuendo.

December 13, 1887

H.L. Loucks, president of the Dakota Farmers' Alliance, addresses alliance members at the organization's annual meeting in Huron. Although Loucks's speech took place two years before statehood, the Farmers' Alliance played an instrumental role in the state's Populist Party, which greatly impacted state politics during the 1890s.

December 14

1935

By a narrow margin of 1,348 to 1,041, members of the Oglala Sioux Tribe of the Pine Ridge Reservation approve the tribe's constitution and bylaws in accordance with the 1934 Indian Reorganization Act.

2001

After 125 years, the Homestake Mining Company mines its last gold ore before ceasing operations.

December 15, 1890

The famous Hunkpapa Lakota chief and holy man Sitting Bull, whose Lakota name was Tatanka Iyotake, is killed along the Grand River by Indian police from the Standing Rock Agency over increasing concerns related to the Ghost Dance. Sitting Bull was originally buried near Fort Yates, North Dakota; however, in 1953, his remains were moved to a burial site west of Mobridge. A large monument memorializes his burial place.

December 16, 1919

Thirteen military veterans conduct the first meeting of what would become the American Legion Roy S. Hickman Post 78 in Leola. The post received its charter the following August 1920.

December 17, 2014

Philanthropist T. Denny Sanford and the State of South Dakota announce plans for a $50 million scholarship program for students attending the state's technical schools. The program involves a $25 million gift from Sanford and a $25 million match from the state. According to the press release, it is anticipated that three hundred scholarships will be awarded during each of the first five years of the program.

December 18, 2015

Teach for America–South Dakota and the Standing Rock Sioux Tribe and Rosebud Sioux Tribe announce an agreement to recruit tribal members to teach at reservation schools. The hope is that more tribal college graduates will be encouraged to become teachers.

December 19, 1940

The State of South Dakota issues a charter to the Codington-Clark Electric Association, Inc. In October, representatives from Codington and Clark Counties met to discuss a joint association that would provide rural electrification. Such associations became possible through the Rural Electrification Administration program under Franklin Roosevelt.

December 20, 1890

L. Frank Baum, editor of the Aberdeen *Saturday Pioneer*, writes an editorial five days after the death of Sitting Bull. In the piece, Baum writes:

> *The Whites, by law of conquest, by justice of civilization, are masters of the American continent, and the best safety of the frontier settlements will be secured by the total annihilation of the few remaining Indians. Why not annihilation? Their glory has fled, their spirit broken, their manhood effaced; better that they die than live the miserable wretches that they are.*

December 21

1965

The site of the December 29, 1890 Wounded Knee Massacre is designated as a National Historic Landmark by the National Park Service. The site is regarded as hallowed ground due to the mass shooting of nearly three hundred Lakota men, women and children by the Seventh Cavalry.

1981

Bear Butte is designated as a National Historic Landmark. In 1961, Bear Butte became a South Dakota state park. Named for its appearance as a silhouette of a bear, it was long called by the Lakota "Mato Paha" (Bear Mountain). Today, it remains a notable landmark in western South Dakota and a religious site for several Indian nations.

December 22, 1915

High rates charged for transporting livestock to Sioux City, Iowa, results in the Sioux City Livestock Exchange filing a complaint against the Chicago, Milwaukee and St. Paul Railway Company. The complaint was originally filed with the South Dakota Railroad Commission; however, since it involved an out-of-state complainant, the commission referred the case to the federal Interstate Commerce Commission.

December 23, 1890

As tensions increase over the Ghost Dance ceremony, Big Foot, also known as Spotted Elk, leads his band from the Cheyenne River Reservation to the Pine Ridge Reservation. Six days later, Big Foot and his people would be massacred by the Seventh Cavalry at Wounded Knee.

December 24, 1969

Assistant Secretary of the Interior Harrison Loesch certifies the Oglala Sioux Tribe's December 4 election results. The election featured several amendments to the Oglala Sioux Tribe's constitution and bylaws, which tribal members approved. According to provisions in the 1934 Indian Reorganization Act, at least 30 percent of the eligible voters had to participate in the election in order for the results to be approved by the Secretary of the Interior's Office.

December 25, 1983

Many holiday travelers had not yet reached their destinations by Christmas morning. A blizzard that started the evening of December 23 stranded hundreds of people. According to the National Weather Service, as many as seventy vehicles were stranded on one fourteen-mile length of Interstate 90.

December 26, 2008

The first Dakota 38 Memorial Ride reaches its destination in Mankato, Minnesota. Riding on horseback, participants start from the Lower Brule

Reservation and spend sixteen days traveling across eastern South Dakota into Minnesota. The planned arrival on December 26 each year memorializes the thirty-eight Dakota Indians who were hanged in Mankato in 1862. They had been convicted because of their involvement in the 1862 Dakota Conflict. The hanging remains the largest public mass execution in U.S. history.

December 27–28, 1996

Captain 11, the longtime KELO-land children's program featuring Dave Dedrick, tapes its last episode. The hour-long segment featured a great deal of fanfare. Although taped on December 27, KELO-land broadcast the final episode twice—once the following day on December 28 and then again on January 1, 1997. *Captain 11* began in 1955 and was on the air for well over forty-one years.

December 28, 1890

The construction of the Fremont, Elkhorn & Missouri Valley Railroad depot highlights the start of Belle Fourche as a new community.

December 29, 1890

The Wounded Knee Massacre, conducted by the U.S. Seventh Cavalry Regiment under the command of Major Samuel M. Whitside, leaves almost three hundred Lakota men, women and children dead. The massacre remains the largest mass shooting in the nation's history.

December 30, 1966

A committee appointed by South Dakota State College president Hilton M. Briggs conducts its first meeting to discuss plans for an agricultural museum.

A little over five months later, the South Dakota State College University Museum opened in the basement of Wenona Hall in May 1967. The origins of the museum, however, actually date to as early as 1884. Today, the museum is known as the South Dakota State Agricultural Heritage Museum.

December 31, 1902

The Hiawatha Asylum for Insane Indians opens in Canton. As the only facility of its kind in the United States, individuals from at least fifty-three Indian nations are sent to the asylum during its existence. An investigation in 1926 by the federal Meriam Commission reported poor conditions and dehumanizing treatment at the facility. However, the Hiawatha Asylum for Insane Indians did not officially close until February 1934.

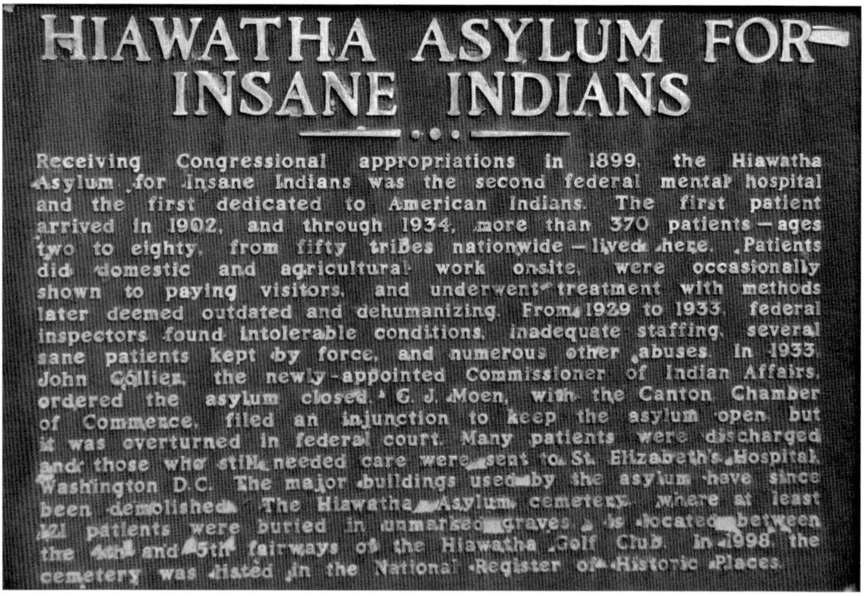

HIAWATHA ASYLUM FOR
INSANE INDIANS

Receiving Congressional appropriations in 1899, the Hiawatha Asylum for Insane Indians was the second federal mental hospital and the first dedicated to American Indians. The first patient arrived in 1902, and through 1934, more than 370 patients – ages two to eighty, from fifty tribes nationwide – lived here. Patients did domestic and agricultural work onsite, were occasionally shown to paying visitors, and underwent treatment with methods later deemed outdated and dehumanizing. From 1929 to 1933, federal inspectors found intolerable conditions, inadequate staffing, several sane patients kept by force, and numerous other abuses. In 1933, John Collier, the newly-appointed Commissioner of Indian Affairs, ordered the asylum closed. G. J. Moen, with the Canton Chamber of Commerce, filed an injunction to keep the asylum open, but it was overturned in federal court. Many patients were discharged and those who still needed care were sent to St. Elizabeth's Hospital, Washington D.C. The major buildings used by the asylum have since been demolished. The Hiawatha Asylum cemetery, where at least 121 patients were buried in unmarked graves, is located between the 4th and 5th fairways of the Hiawatha Golf Club. In 1998, the cemetery was listed in the National Register of Historic Places.

Hiawatha Asylum historical marker. *Brad Tennant.*

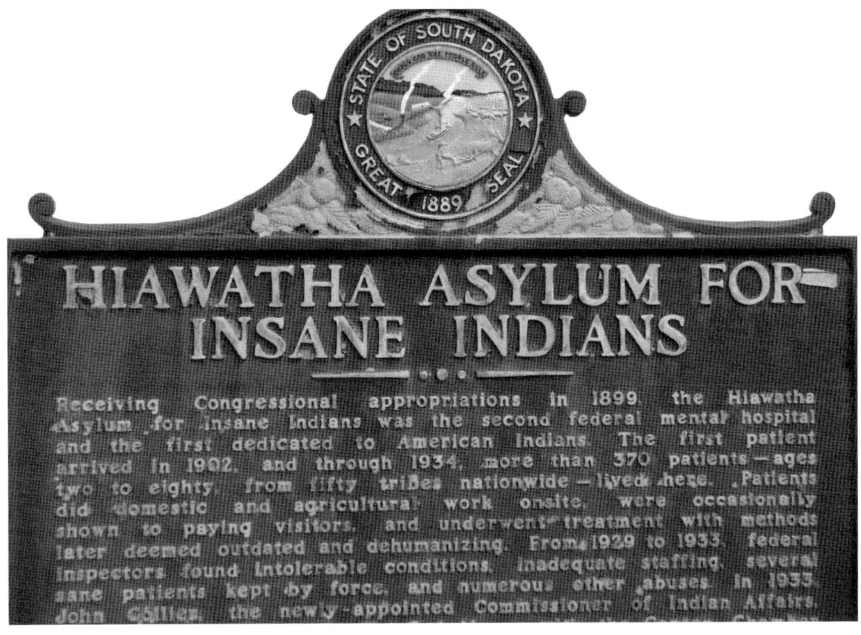

Hiawatha Asylum. *Brad Tennant.*

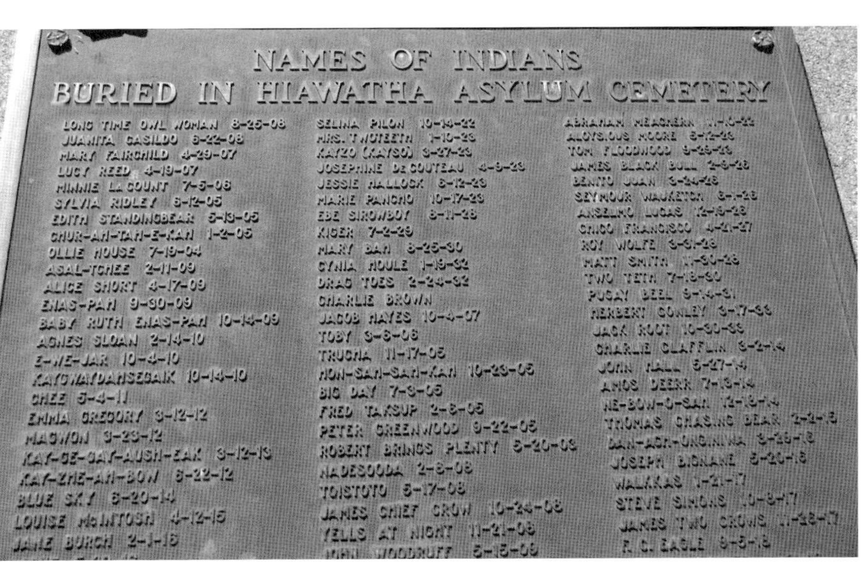

Hiawatha Cemetery Roll. *Brad Tennant.*

Sources

Information included in this book is from a variety of sources. When I began, I knew certain major events that occurred throughout South Dakota history, but there are obviously a fair number of lighter or more trivial events that I found as I was investigating a particular topic. More often than not, one topic would lead me to another. In most cases, I took care in checking and double-checking dates with multiple sources whenever I could. Those listed below are some of the more specific sources used.

Books

Bakken, Stephen C. *The Bet On It! Book of South Dakota Trivia*. Sioux Falls, SD: Ex Machina Publishing Company, 1992.

History Committee of Brown County Museum and Historical Society. *Brown County History*. Aberdeen, SD: North Plains Press, 1980.

Hoover, Herbert T., and Harry F. Thompson. *A New South Dakota History*. Sioux Falls, SD: Center for Western Studies, 2005.

Karl E. Mundt Historical & Educational Foundation. Karl E. Mundt Library, Dakota State University.

Lauck, Jon, John E. Miller and Donald C. Simmons Jr., eds. *The Plains Political Tradition: Essays on South Dakota Political Culture*. Vol. 1. Pierre: South Dakota State Historical Society Press, 2011.

———. *The Plains Political Tradition: Essays on South Dakota Political Culture*. Vol. 2. Pierre: South Dakota State Historical Society Press, 2014.

Nedved, Gregory J. *South Dakota Presidential Trivia*. Pierre, SD: State Publishing Company, 1995.

Popowski, Bert. *South Dakota Brags*. Custer, SD: published by the author, 1953.

Robinson, Doane. *A Brief History of South Dakota*. New York: American Book Company, 1905.

———. *History of South Dakota*. Indianapolis, IN: B.F. Bowen, 1904.

Schell, Herbert S. *History of South Dakota*. 4th ed. Revised by John E. Miller. Pierre: South Dakota State Historical Society Press, 2004.

Sneve, Virginia Driving Hawk, ed. *South Dakota Geographic Names*. Sioux Falls, SD: Brevet Press, 1973.

State of South Dakota. *Public Documents of the State of South Dakota, Being the Annual and Biennial Reports of Various Public Officers and Institutions, to the Governor and Legislature*. Pierre, SD: State Publishing Company, 1907.

Internet

Chicago Daily Tribune. http://chroniclingamerica.loc.gov/lccn/sn84031492/.

Ellsworth Air Force Base. http://www.ellsworth.af.mil.

Mundt, Karl. *Your Washington and You* (newsletter). Karl E. Mundt Historical & Educational Foundation. Karl E. Mundt Library, Dakota State University. http://dlsd.sdln.net/cdm/search/searchterm/Washington.

South Dakota Board of Railroad Commissioners. Annual Report of the Railroad Commissioners of the State of South Dakota for the Year Ending.… Huron, SD: Huronite Printing Company. Multiple years. https://catalog.hathitrust.org/Record/008893478.

About the Author

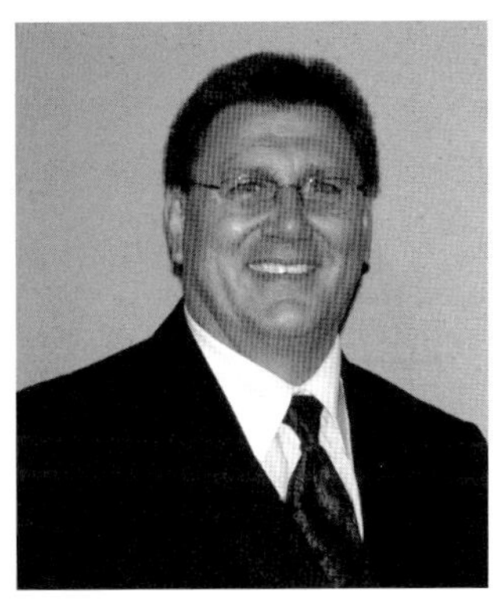

Brad Tennant grew up in Gettysburg, South Dakota, where townships such as Gettysburg, Lincoln and Appomattox reflect the history of the Civil War veterans who settled the area. Although he always had an interest in the state's history, he was fortunate to have Robert Thompson, Dr. Robert Webb and Dr. Arthur Buntin as professors at what is now Northern State University. Even as he began his teaching career, his professors continued to influence him by their involvement in local history-related groups and attendance at history conferences. He has a BS in secondary education and an MA in teaching from Northern State University, both in the areas of history and social science. As a James Madison Fellow, he earned a MA in history from the University of North Dakota and his EdD in history education from the University of South Dakota.

In 1994, Tennant received the Governor's Award for History Teacher of the Year from the South Dakota State Historical Society, and the Center for Western Studies Dakota Conference recognized him with the 2003 "Distinguished Contribution to the Preservation of the Cultural Heritage of South Dakota and the Northern Plains" award. In 2013, he received a gubernatorial appointment to the Commission for South Dakota's 125th Anniversary of Statehood.

About the Author

Tennant is a professor of history and the American Studies Program director at Presentation College in Aberdeen, South Dakota. In addition to his teaching assignments, Tennant is an active researcher, writer and presenter on a variety of state and regional topics. As a gubernatorial appointee, he serves on the board of trustees of the South Dakota State Historical Society. He is also a member of several other national, state and local historical organizations.